Table of Contents

Table of Contents

MASTERING BASIC SKILLS
SECOND GRADE

Brighter Child®
An imprint of Carson-Dellosa Publishing LLC
Greensboro, North Carolina

An imprint of Carson-Dellosa Publishing, LLC
P.O. Box 35665
Greensboro, NC 27425-5665

carsondellosa.com

Printed in the USA. All rights reserved.
ISBN 978-1-4838-0107-0

01-002141151

Introduction

Welcome to *Mastering Basic Skills*. Second grade is the year in elementary school when children begin to make sense of their early academic skills. Most seven- and eight-year-olds are rapidly begining to recognize familiar words, increasing their ability to read new words, and are able to add and subtract with much greater speed. All of the skills learned in first grade are now providing the second grader with a strong foundation on which to build more complicated skills.

Second grade is a fun year, filled with growth. You may notice that your child is more relaxed, has a calmer disposition, and is able to concentrate for longer periods of time. Often, overly active first-grade personalities have grown into more independent children who are ready to take on additional responsibilities and who have reasoning capabilities. Second graders are beginning to recognize the value of money and the importance of time. Your child is growing up and is developing a better sense of self.

Although you will see much academic and behavioral growth, you may also notice that your second grader may sometimes lack confidence, be self-critical, or worry more often. Your child may also prefer not to be singled out in school—even for praise. Once being the center of attention was a great deal of fun—now it can be upsetting and make children feel self-conscious. Second graders better understand people and the world; this understanding provides more maturity but also causes more worries.

In the past, your child may have had lots of playmates, but now, true friendships are being developed. Children are learning more about how people get along with each other and the importance of respecting one another.

Children will welcome the fun of practicing and perfecting their second grade skills. *Mastering Basic Skills* provides children with stories, games, drills, and activities that will enhance and improve their academic skills. Enjoy and participate with your second grader. With *Mastering Basic Skills*, it can be a delightful year!

Everyday Ways to Enrich Learning Experiences

Language Arts

The single most important skill that a child needs for success in school, and later in life, is to be "literate." In other words, children must learn how to read. You can do many things to encourage literacy.

- Read to your child every day and encourage him or her to read to you. Have your child use a different voice for each character in a story.
- Talk about the pictures.
- Ask questions such as who, what, where, when, why, and how about key details in a text.
- Ask your child to guess what is going to happen next.
- Encourage your child to retell favorite stories or favorite parts of a story.
- Have your child write an opinion piece about a book he or she recently read. Discuss the reasons why he or she liked or did not like the book.
- Have your child make up a new ending for a story.
- Go to the library and let your child choose new books. Encourage your child to read a variety of texts, such as fiction, informational, or poetry.
- Write stories together. Have your child illustrate the stories.
- Have your child make a comic book.
- Draw pictures that represent compound words and have your child guess the compound word. For example, draw a bird and a house to have your child guess birdhouse.
- Play listening games. Ask your child to identify words that share the same sound: initial sounds, ending sounds, vowel sounds, and so on.
- Record your child telling a story or reading a poem. Then, listen to the recording together.
- Encourage your child to use describing words during everyday occurrences, like describing dinner.
- Fill your child's environment with literacy materials like magnetic letters, books, magazines, newspapers, catalogs, paper, pencils, crayons, paints, and CDs of children's music.
- Encourage your child to write thank-you notes or letters.
- Together, make a scrapbook of second grade memories.
- Supervise your child's use of the Internet. Search for stories, games, and learning activities that your child can enjoy online.
- Have your child explain how to use a dictionary, glossary, table of contents, and so on.

Math and Science

So many toys and puzzles provide young children with early math and science learning experiences. Remember to point out all the ways we use numbers and science in our daily lives. Here are some suggested activities:

- Provide blocks, puzzles, and other building materials. Have your child describe the different shapes and build objects in two different ways.
- Cut circles and rectangles out of construction paper. Encourage your child to divide them into two, three, or four equal shares and describe the shares using the words halves, thirds, half of, a third of, and so on.
- Encourage play with magnets, scales, and science books and kits.
- Have your child practice adding and subtracting within 20 using mental math. Quiz your child while at the grocery store or while driving around town.
- Play hide and seek with your child. Have your child count out loud by fives, tens, or hundreds while you hide.
- Have your child estimate the length of different objects around the house. Then, have him or her measure the item with a ruler.
- Measure two objects that are different lengths. Ask your child to calculate how much longer one object is than another in terms of a standard length unit.
- Help your child learn basic math facts. Play basic fact games.
- Play card games. This can help children learn to add quickly.
- Have your child pretend to buy snacks or his or her favorite toys. Label each object with an amount and give your child dollar bills, quarters, dimes, nickels, and pennies and encourage him or her to configure the correct amounts to "buy" the items.
- Visit science and children's museums.
- Talk about how we use numbers in the real world: telling time, buying groceries, paying bills, and so on.
- Go on a nature walk with your child. Help him or her gather data during the walk then make a bar graph representing the data. For instance, create a bar graph that shows how many different red, green, yellow, and orange leaves your child found on a walk.
- Get your child a watch and encourage telling time on the hour, on the half hour, and in five-minute intervals.
- Encourage your child to begin a hobby. Encourage individual interests.

Recommended Books for Second Graders

A

Alex and the Cat by Helen V. Griffith
The All New Jonah Twist by Natalie Honeycutt
Amazing Grace by Mary Hoffman
Anatole books by Eve Titus
Angel Child, Dragon Child
    by Michele Maria Surat
Angelina Ballerina by Katharine Holabird
Annie and the Old One by Miska Miles
Annie's Pet by Barbara Brenner
Arthur books by Marc Brown
Aunt Eater's Mystery Vacation
    by Doug Cushman

B

Babar books by Laurent de Brunhoff
A Bear Called Paddington by Michael Bond
Berenstain Bears books by Stan and Jan
    Berenstain
Bernard by Bernard Waber
A Big Fat Enormous Lie by Marjorie Weinman
    Sharmat
Big Goof and Little Goof by Joanna and
    Philip Cole
Big Max by Kin Platt
The Black Snowman by Phil Mendez
Book of Animal Riddles by Bennett Cerf
The Boy with the Helium Head
    by Phyllis Reynolds Naylor
Buggy Riddles by Katy Hall and Lisa Eisenberg

C

Cam Jansen and the Mystery of the Dinosaur
    Bones by David A. Adler
A Chair for My Mother by Vera B. Williams
Chang's Paper Pony by Eleanor Coerr
Circles, Triangles, and Squares by Tana Hoban
Cloudy with a Chance of Meatballs
    by Judi Barrett
Curious George books by H. A. Rey

D

Danny and the Dinosaur by Syd Hoff
The Day Jimmy's Boa Ate the Wash
    by Trinka Hakes Noble
Digging Up Dinosaurs by Aliki
The Dog That Called the Pitch
    by Matt Christopher

E

The Emperor's New Clothes
    by Hans Christian Andersen

F

Freckle Juice by Judy Blume
Frederick by Leo Lionni
Frog and Toad All Year by Arnold Lobel
Frog and Toad Are Friends by Arnold Lobel
The Frog Prince by Alan Trussell-Cullen
Funnybones by Janet and Allan Ahlberg

G

The Gingerbread Boy by Paul Galdone
The Golly Sisters Go West by Betsy Byars
Gorky Rises by William Steig
Grandfather Tang's Story by Ann Tompert
Gregory, the Terrible Eater by Mitchell Sharmat

H

Harry and the Terrible Whatzit
    by Dick Gackenbach
Harry by the Sea by Gene Zion
Harry's Visit by Barbara Ann Porte
Hattie Rabbit by Dick Gackenbach
Henry and Mudge books by Cynthia Rylant
Here Comes the Strikeout by Leonard Kessler
Hooray for the Golly Sisters! by Betsy Byars
Hour of the Olympics by Mary Pope Osborne

I

I Was a Second Grade Werewolf
    by Daniel Pinkwater
If You Give a Moose a Muffin
    by Laura Joffe Numeroff
If You Give a Mouse a Cookie
    by Laura Joffe Numeroff
Imogene's Antlers by David Small

J

Jackie Robinson and the Story of All-Black
    Baseball by Jim O'Connor
Jake and the Copycats by Joanne Rocklin
Jethro and Joel Were a Troll by Bill Peet
John Henry, an American Legend
    by Ezra Jack Keats

Joshua James Likes Trucks by Catherine Petrie
Just a Dream by Chris Van Allsburg
Just for You by Mercer Mayer
Just So Stories by Rudyard Kipling

L

A Light in the Attic by Shel Silverstein
The Little House by Virginia Lee Burton
Little Wolf, Big Wolf by Matt Novak
Lyle, Lyle, Crocodile by Bernard Waber

M

Mag the Magnificent by Dick Gackenbach
Maggie and the Pirate by Ezra Jack Keats
Magic School Bus books by Joanna Cole
Marvin Redpost: Class President
    by Louis Sachar
Miss Nelson Has a Field Day by Harry Allard
    and James Marshall
Miss Nelson Is Missing! by Harry Allard and
    James Marshall
The Mitten: A Ukrainian Folktale, adapted and
    illustrated by Jan Brett
More Riddles by Bennett Cerf
My Father's Dragon by Ruth Gannett
My Name Is María Isabel by Alma Flor Ada
The Mysterious Tadpole by Steven Kellogg

N

Nice New Neighbors by Franz Brandenberg
No Jumping on the Bed! by Tedd Arnold

O

Oink and Pearl by Kay Chorao
Ox-Cart Man by Donald Hall

P

Paul Bunyan, a Tall Tale, retold and illustrated
    by Steven Kellogg
Penrod's Picture by Mary Blount Christian
Petunia by Roger Duvoisin
Picnic with Piggins by Jane Yolen
Pioneer Cat by William H. Hooks
A Pocketful of Cricket by Rebecca Caudill
Polar Express by Chris Van Allsburg

R

Rats on the Roof and Other Stories
    by James Marshall
The Relatives Came by Cynthia Rylant

S

Sleeping Ugly by Jane Yolen
The Smallest Cow in the World
    by Katherine Paterson
Smasher by Dick King-Smith
Soap Soup and Other Verses by Karla Kuskin
Something Queer in the Cafeteria
    by Elizabeth Levy
Song Lee and the Hamster Hunt by Suzy Kline
Stan the Hot Dog Man
    by Ethel and Leonard Kessler
Stories about Rosie by Cynthia Voigt
The Stories Huey Tells by Ann Cameron
The Story about Ping by Marjorie Flack and
    Kurt Wiese
The Story of Ferdinand by Munro Leaf
Stringbean's Trip to the Shining Sea
    by Vera B. Williams
Striped Ice Cream by Joan M. Lexau
The Super Camper Caper
    by John Himmelman
Super Cluck by Jane O'Connor and
    Robert O'Connor

T

Tacky the Penguin by Helen Lester
The Teeny Tiny Woman, retold by
    Jane O'Connor
*The Terrible Thing That Happened at Our
    House* by Marge Blaine
Today Was a Terrible Day by Patricia Reilly Giff

Y

Yoo Hoo, Moon! by Mary Blocksma

Z

The Zabajaba Jungle by William Steig
Zack's Alligator by Shirley Mozelle
Zaza's Big Break by Emily Arnold McCully

Second Grade Skills Checklist

This list is an overview of some of the key skills learned in second grade. When using this list, please keep in mind that the curriculum will vary across the United States, as will how much an individual teacher is able to teach over the course of one year. The list will give you an overview of the majority of second grade skills and assist you in motivating, guiding, and helping your child maintain or even increase skills.

Language Arts/Reading

Recognizes the difference between consonants and vowels ....☐
Recognizes y as a vowel ....☐
Recognizes blends: bl, br, cl, cr, dr, fl, fr, gl, gr, pl, pr, scr, sk, sl, sm,
     sn, sp, spl, spr, st, str, sw, tr, tw ....☐
Recognizes consonant digraphs: ch, sh, th, ng ....☐
Recognizes r-controlled vowels: ar, er, ir, or, ur..☐
Recognizes vowel digraphs: au, aw, ea, oo ....☐
Recognizes diphthongs: oi, oy, ou, ow...☐
Recognizes vowel sounds: ai, ay, ea, ee, oa, ue, ui, ow ....☐
Recognizes hard and soft c and g ....☐
Sounds out words ....☐
Recognizes compound words...☐
Discriminates rhyming words..☐
Recognizes antonyms, synonyms, and homonyms ....☐
Recognizes nouns...☐
Recognizes verbs..☐
Recognizes adjectives...☐
Recognizes pronouns...☐
Recognizes adverbs...☐
Recognizes articles...☐
Recognizes helping verbs...☐
Recognizes subject and predicate ....☐
Knows how to create contractions..☐
Knows how to form plurals with -s and -es and irregular plurals ....☐
Knows how to form singular and plural possessives..☐
Can divide words into syllables ....☐
Can identify the main idea of a story ....☐
Can identify the setting of a story...☐
Can identify the conclusion of a story..☐
Draws illustrations to match sentences..☐
Uses correct punctuation: period, question mark, exclamation point ....☐
Identifies types of sentences...☐
Identifies prefixes and suffixes..☐
Is beginning to read and write for pleasure ....☐

Math

Recognizes odd and even numbers .... ❑
Counts by 2s to 100 .... ❑
Counts by 5s to 100 .... ❑
Counts by 10s to 100 .... ❑
Recognizes numbers to 1,000 .... ❑
Completes simple patterns .... ❑
Reads number words to 100 .... ❑
Can sequence events .... ❑
Names eight basic shapes .... ❑
Can write number sentences using +, –, and = ... ❑
Knows addition facts to 20 .... ❑
Knows subtraction facts to 20 .... ❑
Can read and create a graph .... ❑
Understands place value in the ones place .... ❑
Understands place value in the tens place .... ❑
Understands place value in the hundreds place .... ❑
Performs two-digit addition, no regrouping .... ❑
Performs two-digit subtraction, no regrouping .... ❑
Performs three-digit addition, no regrouping .... ❑
Performs three-digit subtraction, no regrouping .... ❑
Performs two-digit addition, with regrouping .... ❑
Performs two-digit subtraction, with regrouping .... ❑
Performs three-digit addition, with regrouping .... ❑
Performs three-digit subtraction, with regrouping .... ❑
Performs addition with three single-digit addends, no regrouping .... ❑
Performs addition with three single-digit addends, with regrouping .... ❑
Recognizes money: penny, nickel, dime, quarter, half-dollar, dollar .... ❑
Knows the value of penny, nickel, dime, quarter, half-dollar, dollar .... ❑
Can count money using coins in combination .... ❑
Can perform money addition problems using a decimal point .... ❑
Can tell time in five-minute intervals .... ❑
Can check subtraction equations with addition .... ❑
Can measure using inches .... ❑
Can measure using centimeters .... ❑
Can identify and write fractions .... ❑
Uses problem-solving strategies to complete math problems .... ❑

Second Grade Word Lists

Compound Words

afternoon	butterfly	eggshell	headline	northwest	sailboat	sundown
airline	campfire	everybody	homemade	notebook	schoolhouse	sunlight
airplane	campground	everyday	homework	nothing	schoolroom	sunrise
anybody	cannot	everyone	hopscotch	nowhere	seashell	sunset
anyone	carpool	everything	horsefly	outdoors	seashore	sunshine
anyplace	cheeseburger	everywhere	horseman	outside	seaweed	textbook
anything	classmate	eyebrow	horseradish	overcome	sidewalk	toenail
anytime	classroom	eyelid	horseshoe	overhead	snowball	toothbrush
anyway	coffeepot	farmhouse	houseboat	overlook	snowflake	toothpick
anywhere	corncob	firefighter	household	overnight	snowman	turtleneck
backbone	cornfield	firewood	housewife	paintbrush	somebody	weekend
backyard	cowboy	fireworks	inside	pancake	someday	whatever
baseball	cowgirl	flagpole	into	pigtail	somehow	whenever
basketball	cupboard	flashlight	jellyfish	playground	someone	wherever
bathrobe	cupcake	flowerpot	junkyard	policeman	something	whoever
bathroom	daytime	football	lifetime	policewoman	sometime	windpipe
bathtub	dishpan	footprint	lighthouse	ponytail	somewhat	windshield
bedroom	doorbell	footstep	lipstick	popcorn	somewhere	without
bedtime	doorway	forget	lookout	quarterback	southeast	woodsman
beehive	downhill	gingerbread	mailbox	railroad	southwest	yourself
billfold	downstairs	goldfish	mailman	rainbow	spaceship	
birdbath	downtown	grandfather	moonlight	raincoat	springtime	
broomstick	dragonfly	grasshopper	motorcycle	raindrop	starfish	
bulldog	driveway	hairbrush	newspaper	rainfall	steamboat	
bullfrog	drugstore	handshake	nobody	rattlesnake	suitcase	
buttercup	earthquake	handwriting	northeast	rowboat	summertime	

R-Controlled Vowels

ar		er		ir	or		ur
arch	harp	after	rubber	birch	born	porch	burger
ark	jar	brother	serve	bird	chorus	record	burn
arm	large	clerk	shepherd	birth	coral	report	burro
art	marble	clover	sister	chirp	cord	short	burst
bar	march	cover	term	circle	core	snore	church
barber	mark	enter	termite	circus	cork	sport	churn
bark	partner	farmer	verse	dirt	corn	store	curb
barn	party	feather	were	fir	for	stork	curl
car	scarf	fern	winter	firm	forest	storm	curtain
card	sharp	germ		first	fork	story	curve
carpet	smart	hammer		giraffe	form	sword	fur
cart	spark	her		girl	fort	thorn	hurdle
carton	star	herb		shirt	forth	torch	hurry
charge	starch	herd		sir	forty	torn	hurt
charm	tar	hermit		skirt	horn		nurse
chart	target	jerk		squirt	horse		purple
dark	yard	monster		stir	lord		purr
darling	yarn	nerve		swirl	more		purse
dart		percent		third	morning		spur
farm		perch		thirsty	north		turkey
garbage		perform		thirty	oral		turn
garden		perk		twirl	orange		turnip
guitar		person		whirl	order		turtle
hard		pitcher			perform		urge

14

Verbs

ask	chew	float	lick	play	shake	stare	watch
bake	clean	fly	listen	pound	shoot	stir	wrap
balance	climb	frown	look	pour	shut	sweep	write
bathe	close	fry	mail	press	sing	swim	yell
beg	color	grab	make	pull	sit	take	
bite	comb	grow	march	push	skate	talk	
blew	cook	hang	mop	read	skip	tap	
blow	crawl	hit	move	ride	sleep	taste	
bounce	crush	hold	nibble	rip	slide	touch	
break	cut	hop	nod	roll	smell	turn	
brush	dance	hug	open	run	smile	twirl	
bury	dig	juggle	pack	saw	speak	twist	
buy	drag	jump	pat	scream	spend	unbutton	
carry	drink	knock	peel	sell	splash	uncover	
catch	eat	lay	pet	send	squeeze	walk	
chase	feed	leap	plant	sew	stand	wash	

Nouns

Persons

baby	grandfather		
baker	grandmother		
boy	king		
bride	man		
butcher	mother		
children	nurse		
cowboy	parents		
cowgirl	prince		
dentist	queen		
doctor	soldier		
farmer	teacher		
father	woman		
girl			

Places

beach	lake
California	museum
church	New York
circus	office
city	Ohio
factory	park
farm	school
field	station
Florida	store
hospital	woods
island	zoo

Things

alligator	computer	pencil	vase
alphabet	desk	piano	violet
apple	doll	pumpkin	violin
bananas	flower	puzzle	watch
bathtub	frog	radio	window
beehive	hamburger	refrigerator	worm
bike	jar	ring	
brush	key	robin	
bug	kite	shelf	
camera	mailbox	skateboard	
car	monkey	spider	
caterpillar	nest	table	
chair	newspaper	telephone	
chalk	owl	tractor	
clock	pail	tree	

Contractions

not		had	will	is	are	have	other
aren't	isn't	he'd	he'll	he's	they're	I've	I'm
can't	mustn't	I'd	I'll	here's	we're	they've	let's
couldn't	shouldn't	she'd	it'll	it's	you're	we've	
didn't	wasn't	they'd	she'll	she's		you've	
doesn't	won't	we'd	there'll	that's			
don't	wouldn't	who'd	they'll	there's			
hadn't		you'd	we'll	what's			
hasn't			who'll	where's			
haven't			you'll	who's			

Rhyme Time

Match the words that **rhyme**.

cat   ten   cake   jeep

but   big   rice   rake

pig   fog   sheep   cone

hen   rut   bone   flute

log   hat   chute   mice

Addition Facts to 10

Add to solve the problems.

A.	B.	C.	D.	E.	F.
3	2	3	5	3	5
+ 1	+ 2	+ 4	+ 3	+ 3	+ 2

G.	H.	I.	J.
4	2	3	5
+ 5	+ 3	+ 0	+ 5

K.	L.	M.	N.
6	4	1	2
+ 2	+ 0	+ 1	+ 1

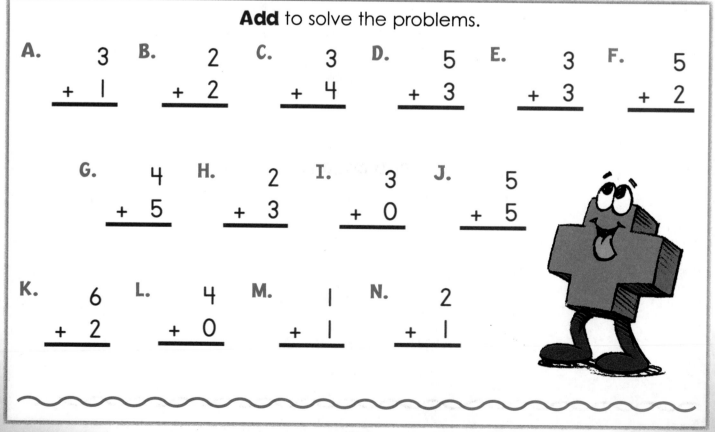

Subtraction Facts to 10

Subtract to solve the problems.

A.   6
  − 5

B.   5
  − 2

C.   8
  − 4

D.   7
  − 6

E.   4
  − 2

F.   9
  − 3

G.   8
  − 6

H.   6
  − 3

I.   3
  − 2

J.   7
  − 5

K.   10
  − 7

Nouns

Write **person**, **place**, or **thing** after each sentence to identify the noun.

1. The children left **school** early today. _____

2. They went to the **park** to play soccer. _____

3. The **teacher** watched the children play. _____

4. A **squirrel** climbed the tree. _____

5. The boys and girls rowed a **boat**. _____

6. One **girl** went down the slide. _____

7. The **boy** was feeding the ducks. _____

8. Two girls were walking their **dog**. _____

Person

Place

Thing

Numeration Review

Count by 10s. Cross out the numbers that do **not** belong.

A. 20, 25, 30, 32, 40, 41, 50, 60, 65, 66, 70

Count by 2s to complete each group of numbers.

B. 2, ___, ___, 8, ___, ___   **C.** 24, ___, 28, ___, ___, 34

Count by 5s. Fill in the blanks with the correct numbers.

D. 5, 10, ___, ___, 25, ___, ___

E. 35, 40, ___, 50, ___, ___, ___

F. 70, ___, 80, ___, ___, ___

G. 60, 65, ___, 75, 80, ___, ___

Write **even** or **odd** after each number.

H. 61 _____   **I.** 13 _____

J. 32 _____   **K.** 29 _____

L. 12 _____   **M.** 88 _____

Finish the Sentence (Nouns)

Complete the sentences by writing **nouns** that make sense on the lines.

1. The _____ drove his _____ through the field.

2. The _____ went to the beach.

3. A nurse works in a _____ .

4. A _____ ran when the alligator moved.

5. My _____ put the _____ in a jar.

6. The _____ belongs to _____ .

7. A _____ tastes very sweet.

8. The _____ broke down in the _____ .

9. The _____ made a lot of _____ .

10. Jamal rode his _____ to the _____ .

Beat the Clock (Addition Facts to 12)

How quickly can you complete this page? Time yourself.
Ready, set, go!

$$\begin{array}{r} 2 \\ + 3 \\ \hline \end{array} \qquad \begin{array}{r} 5 \\ + 5 \\ \hline \end{array} \qquad \begin{array}{r} 1 \\ + 9 \\ \hline \end{array} \qquad \begin{array}{r} 0 \\ + 5 \\ \hline \end{array} \qquad \begin{array}{r} 4 \\ + 3 \\ \hline \end{array} \qquad \begin{array}{r} 3 \\ + 5 \\ \hline \end{array} \qquad \begin{array}{r} 2 \\ + 6 \\ \hline \end{array} \qquad \begin{array}{r} 0 \\ + 9 \\ \hline \end{array}$$

$$\begin{array}{r} 4 \\ + 2 \\ \hline \end{array} \qquad \begin{array}{r} 3 \\ + 8 \\ \hline \end{array} \qquad \begin{array}{r} 2 \\ + 2 \\ \hline \end{array} \qquad \begin{array}{r} 6 \\ + 1 \\ \hline \end{array} \qquad \begin{array}{r} 5 \\ + 2 \\ \hline \end{array} \qquad \begin{array}{r} 6 \\ + 6 \\ \hline \end{array} \qquad \begin{array}{r} 9 \\ + 3 \\ \hline \end{array} \qquad \begin{array}{r} 7 \\ + 2 \\ \hline \end{array}$$

$$\begin{array}{r} 6 \\ + 5 \\ \hline \end{array} \qquad \begin{array}{r} 7 \\ + 4 \\ \hline \end{array} \qquad \begin{array}{r} 3 \\ + 3 \\ \hline \end{array} \qquad \begin{array}{r} 2 \\ + 9 \\ \hline \end{array} \qquad \begin{array}{r} 7 \\ + 5 \\ \hline \end{array} \qquad \begin{array}{r} 7 \\ + 1 \\ \hline \end{array} \qquad \begin{array}{r} 3 \\ + 6 \\ \hline \end{array} \qquad \begin{array}{r} 1 \\ + 1 \\ \hline \end{array}$$

$$\begin{array}{r} 9 \\ + 2 \\ \hline \end{array} \qquad \begin{array}{r} 8 \\ + 4 \\ \hline \end{array} \qquad \begin{array}{r} 8 \\ + 2 \\ \hline \end{array} \qquad \begin{array}{r} 6 \\ + 4 \\ \hline \end{array} \qquad \begin{array}{r} 1 \\ + 4 \\ \hline \end{array} \qquad \begin{array}{r} 4 \\ + 4 \\ \hline \end{array} \qquad \begin{array}{r} 5 \\ + 4 \\ \hline \end{array} \qquad \begin{array}{r} 3 \\ + 7 \\ \hline \end{array}$$

$9 + 3 =$ $7 + 5 =$ $4 + 4 =$ $3 + 6 =$ $6 + 3 =$

$5 + 5 =$ $8 + 2 =$ $7 + 4 =$ $9 + 0 =$ $2 + 4 =$

$0 + 2 =$ $3 + 3 =$ $3 + 8 =$ $2 + 6 =$ $6 + 0 =$

$5 + 4 =$ $8 + 1 =$ $2 + 5 =$ $2 + 2 =$ $9 + 1 =$

$1 + 6 =$ $0 + 0 =$ $4 + 6 =$ $7 + 2 =$ $4 + 3 =$

Time: **Number correct:**

Buried Treasure Math

Look for buried treasure! In each box, write the numeral
you see on the shovel. **Add** to solve each problem.
Draw a picture of treasure inside the treasure chest.

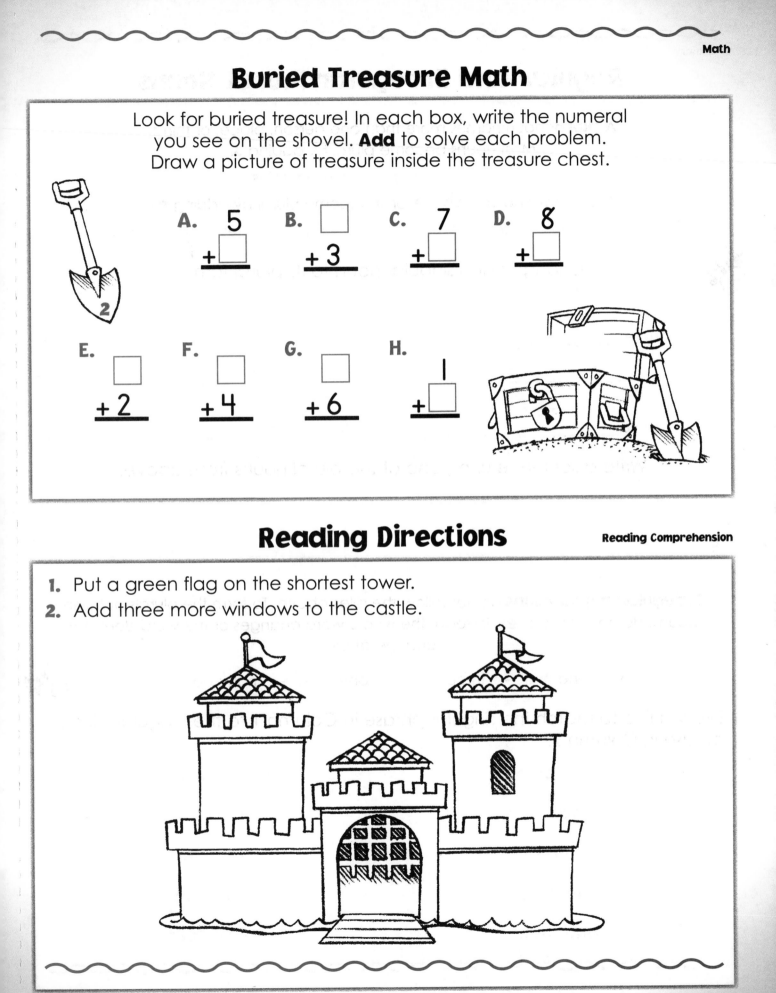

A. 5
$+\square$

B. $\square$
$+3$

C. 7
$+\square$

D. 8
$+\square$

E. $\square$
$+2$

F. $\square$
$+4$

G. $\square$
$+6$

H. 1
$+\square$

Reading Directions

1. Put a green flag on the shortest tower.
2. Add three more windows to the castle.

Regular and Irregular Plural Nouns

A **plural** noun names more than one person, place, or thing.
Most nouns become plural by adding **s**.

book —> book**s**   shirt —> shirt**s**

Nouns that end in **s**, **ch**, **sh**, or **x** become plural by adding **es**.

kiss —> kiss**es**   branch —> branch**es**   wish —> wish**es**   ax —> ax**es**

Change each singular noun to its plural form.

1. picture _____

2. peach _____

3. dish _____

4. fox _____

Write a sentence using one of the plural nouns from above.

5. _____

Irregular plural nouns do not follow the rules above. To form the plurals of these nouns, do not add **s** or **es**. Instead, the whole word changes or the word does not change at all

one **man** —> three **men**   one **deer** —> many **deer**

Draw a line to match the singular phrase in Column 1 to the irregular plural phrase in Column 2.

one tooth	lots of children
one foot	two men
one deer	several teeth
one child	four feet
one man	nine deer

Beat the Clock (Subtraction Facts to 12)

How quickly can you complete this page? Time yourself.
Ready, set, go!

12	10	11	7	12	11	10	12
− 5	− 7	− 4	− 5	− 4	− 9	− 2	− 8

9	7	11	12	12	8	9	9
− 3	− 3	− 5	− 7	− 3	− 7	− 6	− 2

6	10	12	8	9	9	10	11
− 3	− 3	− 9	− 2	− 7	− 5	− 5	− 7

11	11	10	10	11	12	11	7
− 2	− 6	− 8	− 6	− 8	− 6	− 1	− 4

9 − 4 =   7 − 6 =   4 − 4 =   3 − 2 =   6 − 4 =

5 − 5 =   8 − 0 =   7 − 1 =   9 − 8 =   2 − 1 =

0 − 0 =   3 − 1 =   8 − 4 =   2 − 1 =   6 − 2 =

5 − 4 =   8 − 3 =   5 − 1 =   8 − 5 =   9 − 1 =

6 − 1 =   0 − 0 =   6 − 4 =   7 − 2 =   4 − 3 =

Time: **Number correct:**

Verbs

Write the correct **verb** from the word list under each picture.

Word List

swim
yawn
sleep
run
dig
splash
rain
box

Missing Numerals

Write the **missing numerals** in each row.

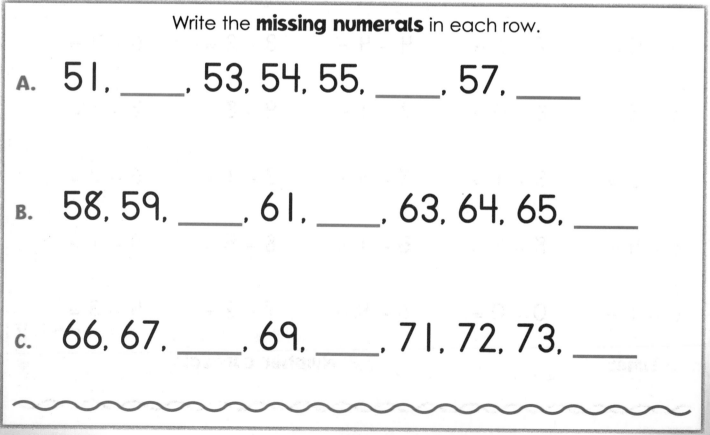

A. 51, ___, 53, 54, 55, ___, 57, ___

B. 58, 59, ___, 61, ___, 63, 64, 65, ___

C. 66, 67, ___, 69, ___, 71, 72, 73, ___

Addition Facts to 20

Add to solve each problem.

A. $9 + 5 =$ ☐   B. $6 + 7 =$ ☐   C. $8 + 3 =$ ☐

D. $10 + 3 =$ ☐   E. $7 + 9 =$ ☐   F. $12 + 8 =$ ☐

G.
$$\begin{array}{r} 9 \\ + 9 \\ \hline \end{array}$$
☐

H.
$$\begin{array}{r} 4 \\ + 8 \\ \hline \end{array}$$
☐

I.
$$\begin{array}{r} 6 \\ + 5 \\ \hline \end{array}$$
☐

J.
$$\begin{array}{r} 7 \\ + 8 \\ \hline \end{array}$$
☐

Noun or Verb?

Decide if each word is a noun or a verb.
Write **noun** or **verb** on the line.

1. horse _____

2. run _____

3. baker _____

4. tree _____

5. car _____

6. boy _____

7. lawn _____

8. see _____

9. grow _____

10. barn _____

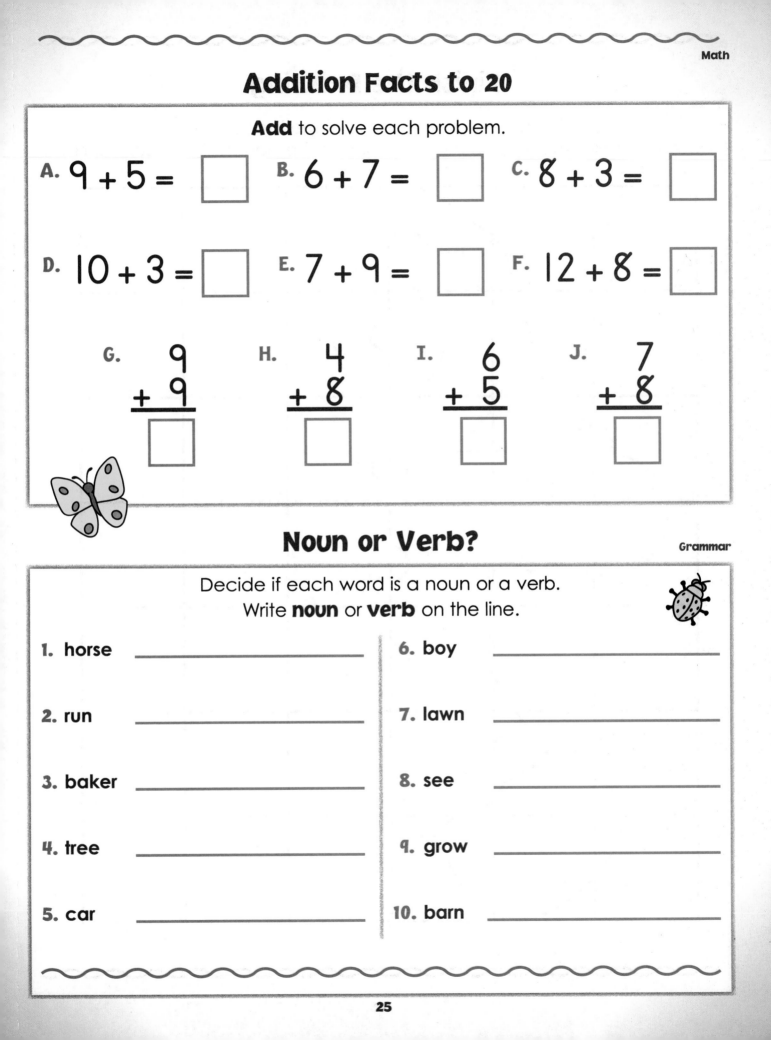

Finish the Drawing

Finish the drawing of the gingerbread boy.
Use the boxes to help you make a copy of the part that is already drawn.

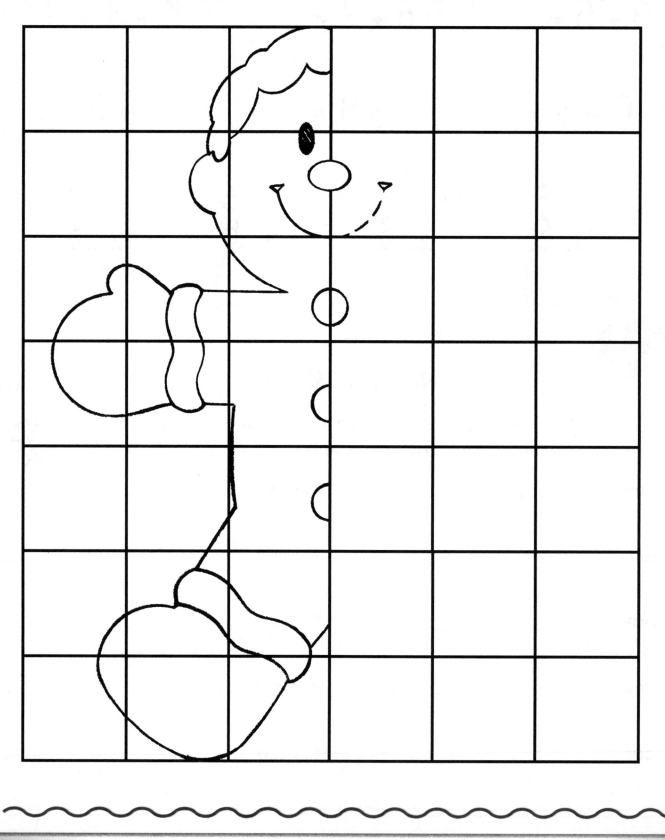

Present and Past Tense

A **present tense** verb tells about action that is happening now.
It also tells about things that happen often or on a regular basis.

I walk home.   Sandy bakes cookies for Christmas.

A **past tense** verb tells about action that has already happened.
The letters **ed** or **d** are usually added to change a verb to the past tense.

I walked home.   I baked cookies yesterday.

Read each sentence. Write **present** if the verb is in the present tense.
Write **past** if the verb is in the past tense.

1. We played a game. _____

2. She twirls her hair. _____

3. I like noodles. _____

4. Amy talked to me. _____

Create Your Own Addition Problems

Write and solve five addition problems.
Answers should be between **11** and **18**.

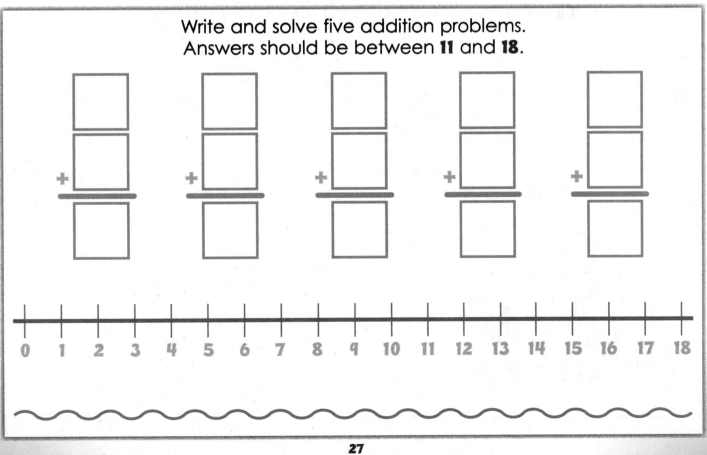

Helping Verbs

A **helping verb** is sometimes used to add meaning to
another verb in a sentence. Some helping verbs include:
can, could, does, did, have, has, is, are, might, will, and **would.**

They **are** playing baseball.   You **can** run very fast!

Complete each sentence with a helping verb from the word list.

Word List   **are**   **can**   **have**   **is**

1. Sue _____ tie her shoes.   2. We _____ going to the store.

3. I _____ cleaned my room.   4. Mrs. Vasquez _____ helping us.

Underline the helping verb in each sentence.
Circle the verb that comes after the helping verb.

5. Shonda was calling your name.   6. I am going to the movies.

7. We are playing in the rain.   8. They were running home.

9. Peter might go to the pool today.   10. We could eat our dinner.

Circle the correct helping verb in each sentence.

11. He (**can   am**) come to my house.

12. My dog (**do   has**) dug a hole in
the backyard.

13. We (**was   were**) singing the songs.

14. Sara (**is   are**) dancing to the music.

28

Dot-to-Dot Math

Subtract. Connect the dots in order from smallest to largest.

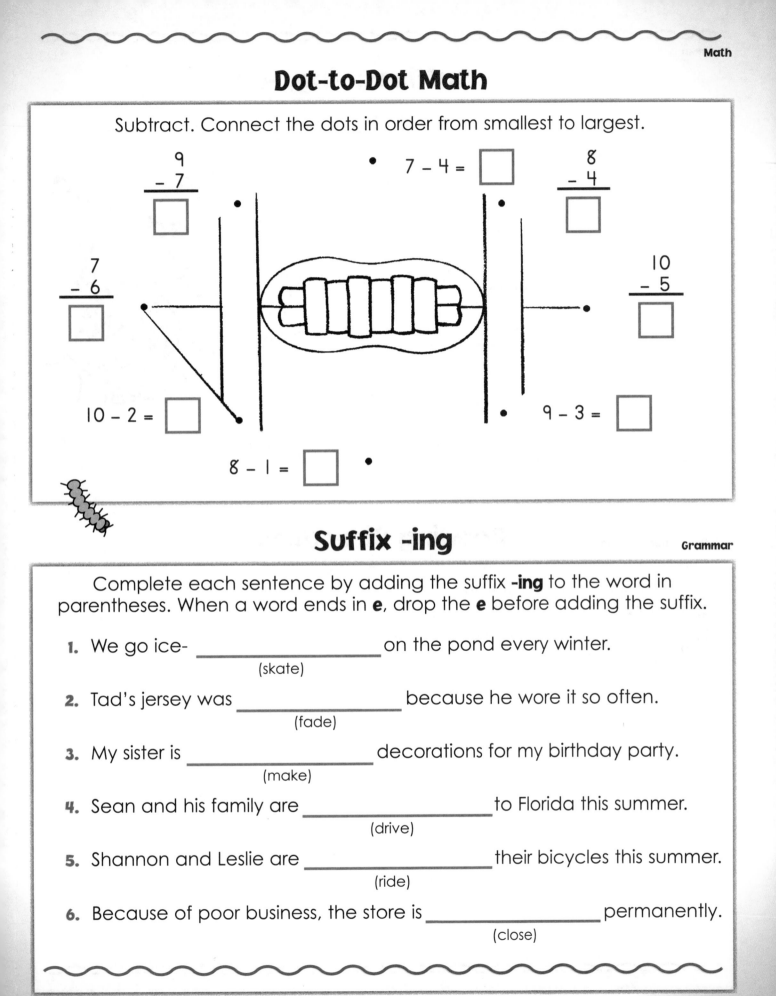

$$\begin{array}{r} 9 \\ -\ 7 \\ \hline \square \end{array}$$

• 7 – 4 = □

$$\begin{array}{r} 8 \\ -\ 4 \\ \hline \square \end{array}$$

$$\begin{array}{r} 7 \\ -\ 6 \\ \hline \square \end{array}$$

$$\begin{array}{r} 10 \\ -\ 5 \\ \hline \square \end{array}$$

10 – 2 = □

9 – 3 = □

8 – 1 = □

Suffix -ing

Complete each sentence by adding the suffix **-ing** to the word in parentheses. When a word ends in **e**, drop the **e** before adding the suffix.

1. We go ice- _____ on the pond every winter.
   (skate)

2. Tad's jersey was _____ because he wore it so often.
   (fade)

3. My sister is _____ decorations for my birthday party.
   (make)

4. Sean and his family are _____ to Florida this summer.
   (drive)

5. Shannon and Leslie are _____ their bicycles this summer.
   (ride)

6. Because of poor business, the store is _____ permanently.
   (close)

Suffixes: -ing, -ed

Write the correct suffix **ing** or **ed** on each line.

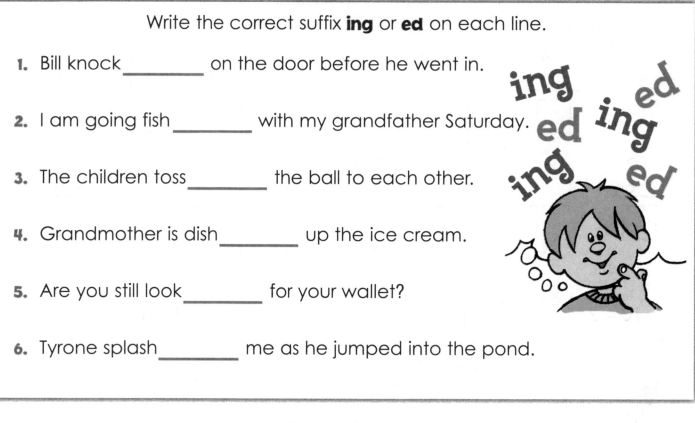

1. Bill knock_____ on the door before he went in.

2. I am going fish_____ with my grandfather Saturday.

3. The children toss_____ the ball to each other.

4. Grandmother is dish_____ up the ice cream.

5. Are you still look_____ for your wallet?

6. Tyrone splash_____ me as he jumped into the pond.

Reading Directions

1. Draw a house and a tree.
2. Color the house red.
3. Draw and color one bird under the tree.
4. Draw a sun. Color it yellow.

Timed Test (Addition Facts to 20)

A.	4 + 4	2 + 0	6 + 3	0 + 2	1 + 4	9 + 4	5 + 6	3 + 5	0 + 7	8 + 3
B.	1 + 0	10 +10	8 + 8	2 + 6	4 + 3	5 + 3	1 + 3	6 + 2	7 + 0	4 + 2
C.	8 + 2	0 + 6	7 + 1	3 + 4	1 + 9	7 + 8	6 + 5	2 + 5	9 + 1	0 + 0
D.	2 + 4	5 + 2	1 + 8	8 + 7	5 + 7	0 + 5	11 + 9	4 + 1	3 + 6	8 + 1
E.	6 + 4	3 + 3	7 + 9	0 + 1	5 + 0	2 + 3	8 + 0	1 + 2	7 + 7	4 + 9
F.	4 + 0	1 + 1	10 + 8	9 + 3	2 + 9	9 + 9	4 + 6	9 + 0	1 + 7	9 + 5
G.	5 + 9	2 + 8	7 + 6	3 + 9	8 + 6	0 + 8	6 + 1	3 + 1	7 + 5	6 + 8
H.	7 + 2	4 + 5	2 + 7	6 + 7	1 + 6	9 + 2	3 + 8	8 + 5	10 + 9	6 + 0
I.	0 + 3	8 + 9	5 + 1	10 +10	9 + 8	5 + 4	2 + 2	9 + 6	7 + 4	4 + 8
J.	5 + 5	1 + 5	9 + 7	4 + 7	2 + 1	7 + 3	0 + 4	8 + 4	6 + 6	3 + 7

Time: _____   **Number correct:** _____

Fact Families

Solve each problem. Draw a line to match the related facts.

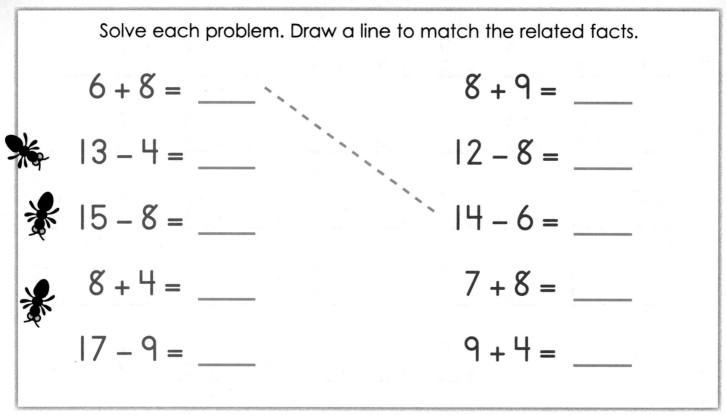

6 + 8 = ____   8 + 9 = ____

13 – 4 = ____   12 – 8 = ____

15 – 8 = ____   14 – 6 = ____

8 + 4 = ____   7 + 8 = ____

17 – 9 = ____   9 + 4 = ____

Short ă

Write the word. Draw the ⌣ symbol over the short vowel sound.

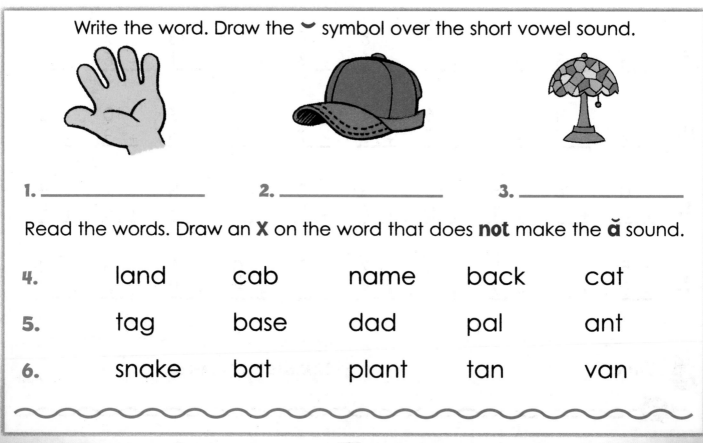

1. _____   2. _____   3. _____

Read the words. Draw an **X** on the word that does **not** make the **ă** sound.

4. land   cab   name   back   cat

5. tag   base   dad   pal   ant

6. snake   bat   plant   tan   van

Adjectives

Some sentences contain words that describe nouns.
These words are called **adjectives**.

He is a nice person.   **The blue sky is pretty.**

Complete each sentence by writing an adjective from the word list.

Word List   yellow   fluffy   strong

1. The _____ school bus drove down the street.

2. A _____ wind blew through the trees.

3. The _____ dog followed me home.

4. Write an adjective to describe you. _____

5. Write an adjective to describe ice cream. _____

6. Write an adjective to describe your school. _____

7. Write an adjective to describe a bug. _____

8. Write an adjective to describe the playground. _____

Timed Test (Subtraction Facts to 20)

A.
2	17	9	7	16	10	4	12	8	6
− 0	− 8	− 8	− 0	− 9	− 6	− 4	− 6	− 6	− 2

B.
9	5	8	1	11	6	13	7	3	9
− 1	− 4	− 2	− 1	− 5	− 6	− 4	− 7	− 0	− 4

C.
11	18	6	14	20	4	17	10	9	5
− 7	− 9	− 1	− 5	− 8	− 0	− 9	− 1	− 7	− 1

D.
5	10	4	10	9	20	9	8	7	11
− 0	− 2	− 2	− 5	− 0	− 3	− 3	− 8	− 4	− 9

E.
8	3	10	9	6	13	12	1	12	11
− 3	− 1	− 7	− 6	− 5	− 6	− 5	− 0	− 9	− 2

F.
9	8	7	11	13	8	3	15	8	2
− 9	− 7	− 6	− 4	− 8	− 5	− 3	− 6	− 1	− 2

G.
7	9	14	20	12	10	6	11	10	6
− 1	− 2	− 7	− 0	− 8	− 4	− 0	− 8	− 9	− 4

H.
20	7	5	13	16	8	15	4	14	12
− 6	− 5	− 2	− 7	− 8	− 0	− 8	− 3	− 9	− 3

I.
3	15	12	15	7	2	16	20	14	10
− 2	− 9	− 4	− 7	− 3	− 1	− 7	− 9	− 6	− 8

J.
10	5	12	8	4	11	9	14	6	13
− 3	− 5	− 7	− 4	− 1	− 3	− 5	− 8	− 3	− 5

Time: **Number correct:**

Cookbook for Kids

Note: Anytime children "cook" in a kitchen, adult supervision is required.

1

Table of Contents

Pizza Snacks

What you need:

4 Triscuit® crackers, 4 tablespoons tomato sauce or ketchup, 1 slice of meat of your choice, and grated mozzarella cheese.

What you do:

Spread the sauce on the crackers. Place one piece of meat on each cracker and sprinkle with cheese. Heat in 325°F oven until the cheese melts. This is a healthy afternoon snack!

Lunch Pizzas

What you need:

7 1/2 ounce can of biscuits, 1/2 cup tomato sauce or ketchup, 2/3 cup cooked ham or pepperoni, and grated mozzarella cheese.

What you do:

With fingers, flatten the biscuit dough on a cookie sheet. Spread sauce on each biscuit. Add meat and sprinkle with cheese. Bake according to the directions on the biscuit package.

3

Fruit Cooler

What you need:

6 ice cubes; 1 orange, peeled and cut into bite-size pieces; 1 banana cut into small chunks; and 12 ounces of a clear carbonated beverage.

What you do:

Place the ice, orange pieces, and banana chunks in a blender and mix until smooth. Pour in the carbonated beverage and mix again. What a yummy taste treat!

Banana Smoothie

What you need:

1 cup plain or vanilla yogurt, 1 banana, ¼ cup apple juice, ⅓ cup strawberries, and 3 ice cubes.

What you do:

Place all the ingredients in a blender and mix well. This is a healthy drink that children love!

2

Trail Mix

What you need:

1 cup peanuts, 1 cup cashews, 1 cup raisins, 1 cup banana chips, and 1 cup mixed dried fruit.

What you do:

Place all the ingredients in a bowl and mix together. Store in a large resealable plastic bag. Serve in small paper cups or in plastic sandwich bags.

Outside Snacks

What you need:

1 cup chocolate chips, 1 cup raisins, 1 cup cereal, and 1 cup candy-covered chocolates.

What you do:

Place all the ingredients in a bowl and mix together. Store in a large resealable plastic bag. Serve in small paper cups or in plastic sandwich bags.

Extra Fun:

Hollow out an apple and fill it with either of these mixes.

4

Chocolate Popcorn

What you need:

6 cups popped popcorn, 1 tablespoon butter, 2 tablespoons corn syrup, 1 tablespoon cocoa powder, 1 tablespoon milk, and salt to taste.

What you do:

Pop the popcorn and keep warm in a low oven. Melt the butter over low heat. Add corn syrup, milk, salt, and cocoa powder to the butter. Stir until mixed well and hot. Pour over the popcorn and mix with a large spoon. Yum!

Popcorn Balls

What you need:

5 to 6 cups popped popcorn, ¼ cup honey, and ¼ cup smooth peanut butter.

What you do:

Pop the popcorn and place in a large pan. Keep the popcorn warm in the oven. In a small pan, boil the honey for 1 to 2 minutes and then add the peanut butter. Stir quickly. Pour over the warm popcorn and mix quickly with a spoon. Be careful—it will be hot. Mold into ball shapes and wrap in wax paper.

Finger Gelatin

What you need:

2 envelopes unflavored gelatin, 2 envelopes flavored gelatin, 2 cups hot water, and 2 cups cold water.

What you need:

Bring 2 cups of water to a boil. Add both the flavored and unflavored gelatins. Mix well. Add the cold water. Pour into a shallow pan and chill until firm. Cut into squares or let your child use cookie cutters to create fun shapes.

Heavenly Pudding

What you need:

1 package chocolate pudding and vanilla ice cream. (Whipped cream may be substituted for the ice cream.)

What you need:

Prepare the pudding according to directions on the package. Once the pudding is firm, add a small scoop of vanilla ice cream or whipped cream to the center of the pudding. This is always a favorite treat of young children!

Sweet Peanut Butter and Raisins

What you need:

2 bread slices, 1½ tablespoons peanut butter, and 1½ tablespoons chopped raisins. (Chopped apples may be substituted for the raisins.)

What you do:

Spread the peanut butter on one slice of bread. Sprinkle the chopped raisins or apples on top of the peanut butter. Top with another piece of bread.

Ham and Cheese Special

What you need:

1 can refrigerated crescent rolls, 2 cups chopped ham, 1 cup grated cheese, and butter.

What you do:

Place the crescent rolls on a cookie sheet. Spread with butter. Sprinkle the center of each roll with ham and cheese. Roll up. Bake according to the directions on the crescent roll package.

6

Chocolate Cookies

What you need:

1 chocolate cake mix, 2 eggs, ⅔ cup vegetable oil, 1 teaspoon vanilla, and chocolate chips.

What you do:

Mix all the ingredients together. Place round spoonfuls on a cookie sheet. Bake at 375°F for about 10 minutes or until the bottom of the cookies begin to brown.

Yummy Tarts

What you need:

1 cup flour, ⅓ cup shortening, 2 tablespoons water, and strawberry preserves.

What you do:

Mix together flour and shortening until creamy. Add water and mix again. Roll into small balls and place in the bottom of a muffin tin. Press the center of the dough with your thumb. Bake at 350°F for approximately 8 minutes. Cool and fill the center of the muffin with the strawberry preserves.

Number Words to 100

Numbers can be written as numerals or as words.

4	18	52	99
four	eighteen	fifty-two	ninety-nine

Draw a line to match each number word to the correct numeral.

A.			B.	
twenty-three	99		fifteen	100
seventy-five	11		eighty-four	84
sixty-two	23		forty-seven	12
ninety-nine	32		twenty-six	15
eighteen	18		fifty-three	47
thirty-two	62		twelve	53
eleven	75		one hundred	26

Missy and Kim: A Story

Read the story. Match the question with the correct answer.

One cold, winter day Missy and Kim went for a walk in the woods. They saw a deer eating the bark of a tree. When Kim stepped on a twig, the deer suddenly ran away. The girls decided it was too cold to keep walking. They went home.

1. Who went for a walk?   the woods

2. What season was it?   Missy and Kim

3. What did the deer eat?   It was too cold.

4. Where did the girls go for a walk?   winter

5. Why did the girls go home?   bark of a tree

Short ě

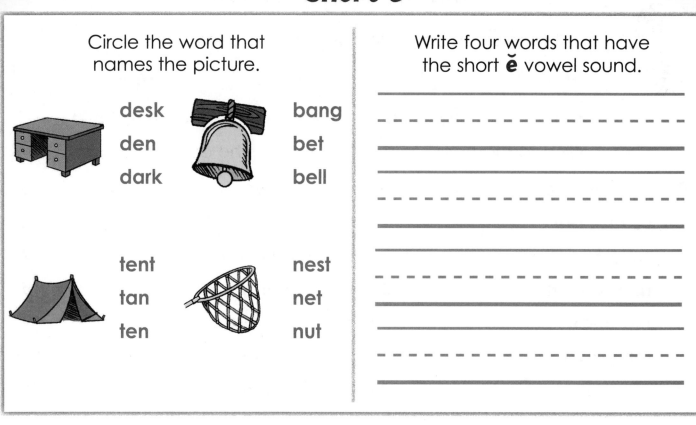

Circle the word that names the picture.

desk
den
dark

bang
bet
bell

tent
tan
ten

nest
net
nut

Write four words that have the short ě vowel sound.

_____

- - - - - - - - - - - - - - - - -

_____

- - - - - - - - - - - - - - - - -

_____

- - - - - - - - - - - - - - - - -

_____

- - - - - - - - - - - - - - - - -

_____

Math

Tic-Tac-Toe Math

Solve the problems. Find three answers in a row that match.

+

12 + 5	8 + 8	10 + 5
6 + 6	8 + 7	8 + 2
9 + 6	9 + 5	6 + 6

−

11 − 7	12 − 6	10 − 9
9 − 4	10 − 5	11 − 6
18 − 9	11 − 9	10 − 7

Addition Chart

Find the sums to complete the chart.

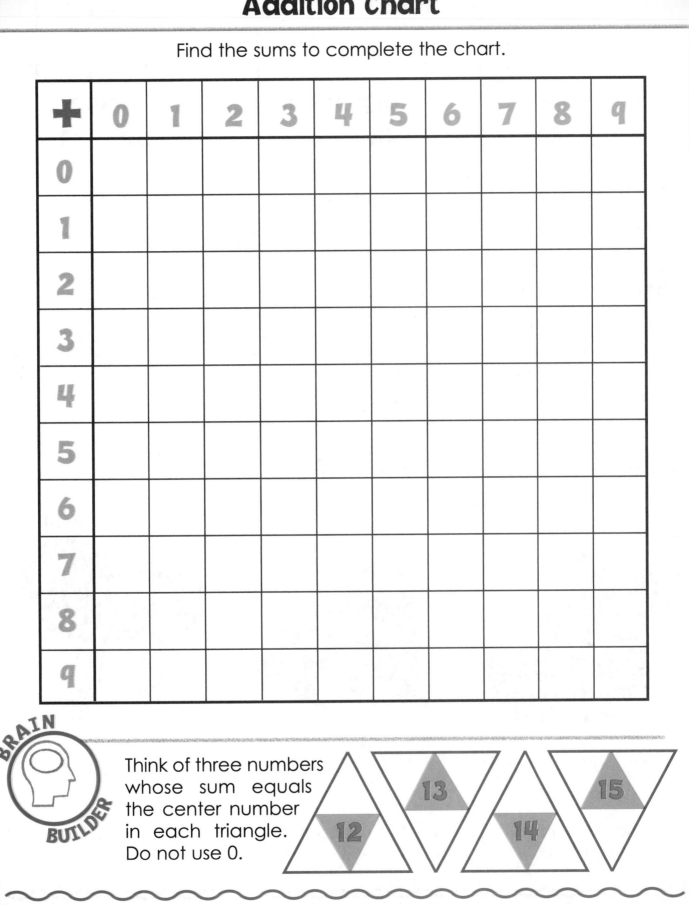

+	0	1	2	3	4	5	6	7	8	9
0										
1										
2										
3										
4										
5										
6										
7										
8										
9										

BRAIN BUILDER

Think of three numbers whose sum equals the center number in each triangle. Do not use 0.

13 15

12 14

Number Words

Circle the correct numeral for each number word.

A. forty-five
54   45

B. eighty-one
18   81

C. three
30   3

D. fifty-eight
58   85

E. thirty
30   31

F. fifteen
15   50

BONUS Write the number words for the following numerals:
0, 20, 30, 40, 60, and 80.

_____   _____   _____

_____   _____   _____

Main Idea

Circle the main idea of each picture.

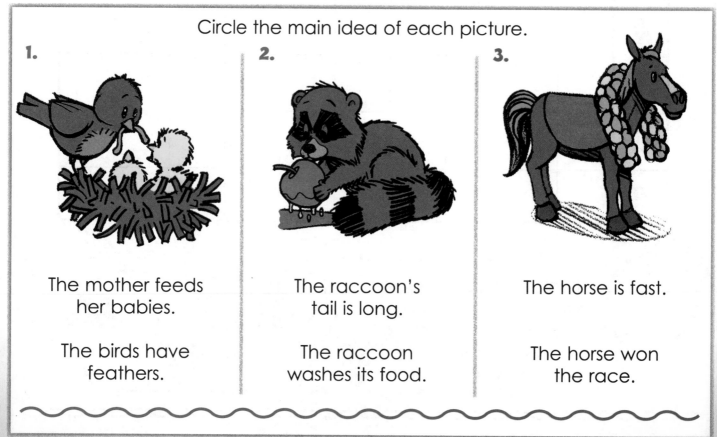

1.
The mother feeds her babies.

The birds have feathers.

2.
The raccoon's tail is long.

The raccoon washes its food.

3.
The horse is fast.

The horse won the race.

Alphabetical Order

Read the words in each jar.
Write the words in alphabetical order on the lines below the jar.

nut
arm
foot
coat
basket

match
whale
cape
yard
shark

1. _____

2. _____

3. _____

4. _____

5. _____

1. _____

2. _____

3. _____

4. _____

5. _____

Adding Three Single-Digit Addends

Add to solve each problem.

A.
$$\begin{array}{r} 1 \\ 3 \\ + 6 \\ \hline 10 \end{array}$$
4

B.
$$\begin{array}{r} 5 \\ 3 \\ + 4 \\ \hline \end{array}$$

C.
$$\begin{array}{r} 1 \\ 9 \\ + 6 \\ \hline \end{array}$$

D.
$$\begin{array}{r} 3 \\ 6 \\ + 3 \\ \hline \end{array}$$

E.
$$\begin{array}{r} 9 \\ 3 \\ + 5 \\ \hline \end{array}$$

F.
$$\begin{array}{r} 1 \\ 6 \\ + 7 \\ \hline \end{array}$$

G.
$$\begin{array}{r} 5 \\ 6 \\ + 4 \\ \hline \end{array}$$

H.
$$\begin{array}{r} 2 \\ 7 \\ + 5 \\ \hline \end{array}$$

I.
$$\begin{array}{r} 4 \\ 1 \\ + 5 \\ \hline \end{array}$$

J.
$$\begin{array}{r} 6 \\ 2 \\ + 7 \\ \hline \end{array}$$

Complete the Sentence

Choose the best adjective from the word list to complete each sentence.

Word List

funny
six
red
hard
oak
flying
furry

1. His kite got caught in that _____ tree.

2. I can't believe you ate _____ hot dogs!

3. At the circus, we laughed at the _____ clowns.

4. Jackie got a _____ bike for Christmas.

5. My pillow is very _____ and lumpy.

6. The rabbits all had soft and _____ ears.

Subject and Predicate

Draw a line to connect the subject and predicate phrases
in each set to form sentences that make sense.

1. The strong winds
2. Our class
3. The spy

A. uprooted three trees.
B. decoded the message.
C. will visit the fire station.

1. My little brother
2. The bumblebee
3. We

A. have fun in art class.
B. fell off his skateboard.
C. stung my sister.

Short ĭ

Print an **i** in each word. Read the word. Draw a short ⌣ symbol over each **i**.

1. w___ g
2. p___ n
3. p___ g
4. f___ sh

Fill in the correct word from the word list to complete each sentence.

Word List

six

ink

kiss

1. The pen ran out of _____.

2. The boy gave the girl a _____.

3. I have _____ marbles.

Tall Sums

Add to solve each problem.

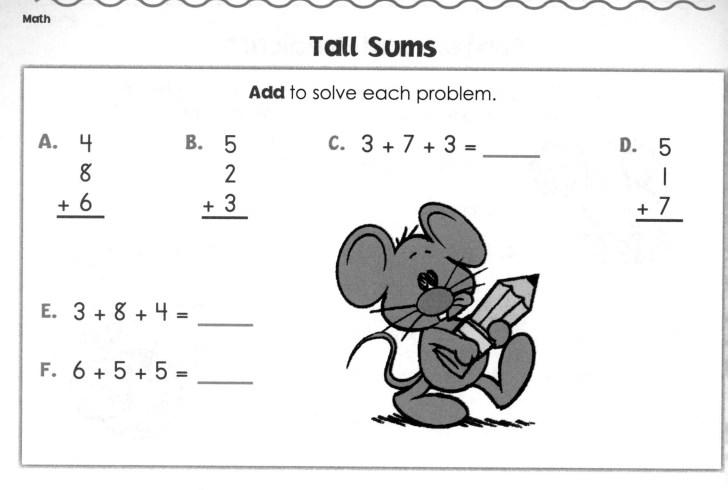

A.   4
       8
   + 6
      ____

B.   5
       2
   + 3
      ____

C.   3 + 7 + 3 = _____

D.   5
       1
   + 7
      ____

E.   3 + 8 + 4 = _____

F.   6 + 5 + 5 = _____

Write Your Own Subject Phrase

Add a **subject phrase** to complete each sentence.

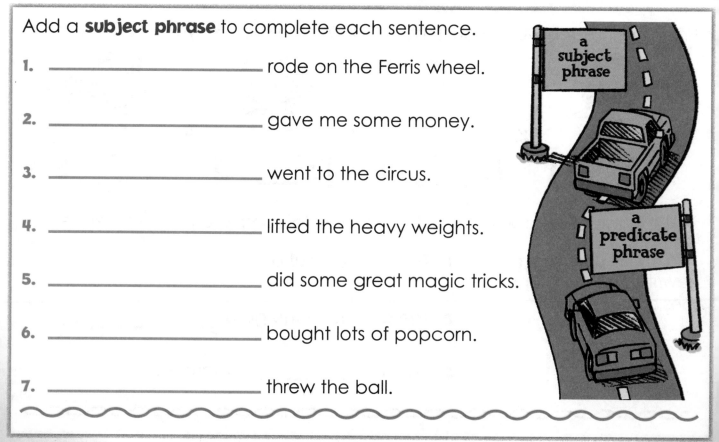

1. _____ rode on the Ferris wheel.

2. _____ gave me some money.

3. _____ went to the circus.

4. _____ lifted the heavy weights.

5. _____ did some great magic tricks.

6. _____ bought lots of popcorn.

7. _____ threw the ball.

Place Value (Tens)

Numbers with two digits can be grouped into sets of tens and ones.

15

is the same as

1 ten and 5 ones

Circle each group of ten. Count how many ones are left over. Write the correct numbers.

A.

17 is_____ten and_____ones

B.

24 is_____tens and_____ones

Group each number into tens and ones.

C. **45** is__4__tens and__5__ones   **D.** **7** is_____tens and_____ones

E. **29** is_____tens and_____ones   **F.** **23** is_____tens and_____ones

G. **4** is_____tens and_____ones   **H.** **99** is_____tens and_____ones

Read the number at the beginning of each row.

Rewrite each number as tens and ones.

I.

	tens	ones
6	0	6
45	4	5
32		
8		
75		

J.

	tens	ones
27		
51		
90		
5		
3		

Math

Two-Digit and One-Digit Addition (No Regrouping)

Rewrite each number sentence in **tens** and **ones** columns.

A. 24 + 2 = 26   **B.** 15 + 1 = 16   **C.** 72 + 5 = 77   **D.** 31 + 8 = 39

tens	ones
2	4
+	2
2	6

tens	ones
+	

tens	ones
+	

tens	ones
+	

Add to find the sum. Remember to add numbers in the ones place first.

E. 21
+ 5

F. 55
+ 4

G. 37
+ 1

H. 64
+ 3

I. 91
+ 7

J. 40
+ 3

K. 81
+ 8

L. 11
+ 5

M. 46
+ 2

N. 29
+ 0

O. 62
+ 4

Grammar

Double Consonant Syllables

Complete each word using a consonant pair from the box.
Draw a line to divide each word into syllables.

pp   tt   gg   ll   dd   nn   bb   zz   mm

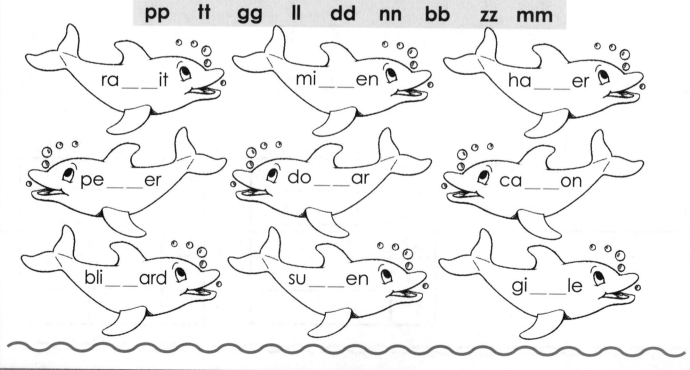

ra___it   mi___en   ha___er

pe___er   do___ar   ca___on

bli___ard   su___en   gi___le

Short ŏ

Print an **o** on each line. Say the word. Draw a short ˘ symbol over each **o**.

1. l__g

2. t__p

3. b__x

4. fr__g

5. p__t

6. d__g

Read the words. Draw an **X** on the word that does not have the short ŏ sound.

7. note   pop   shop   mom   Tom

8. hop   hog   stop   broke   song

Double-Digit Addition

Add to solve each problem.

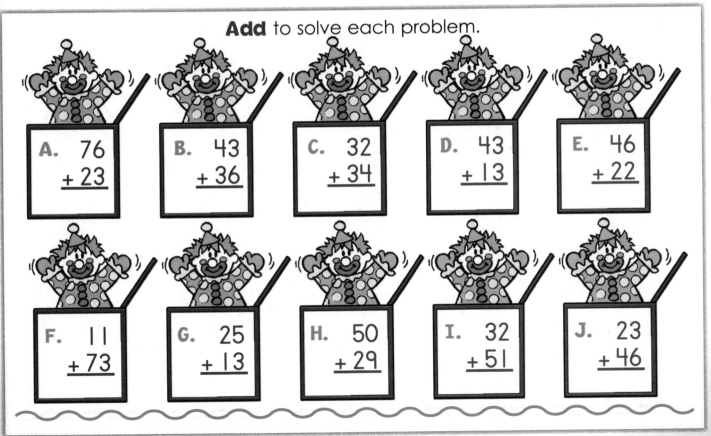

A. 76
+ 23

B. 43
+ 36

C. 32
+ 34

D. 43
+ 13

E. 46
+ 22

F. 11
+ 73

G. 25
+ 13

H. 50
+ 29

I. 32
+ 51

J. 23
+ 46

Color by Code

Add or **subtract**. Use the code to color the picture.

56 = yellow

33 = brown

94 = green

77 = blue

49 = red

$$\begin{array}{r} 32 \\ +\ 24 \\ \hline \end{array}$$

$$56 - 23 =$$

$$32 + 62 =$$

$$\begin{array}{r} 89 \\ -\ 33 \\ \hline \end{array}$$

$$22 + 11 =$$

$$\begin{array}{r} 25 \\ +\ 24 \\ \hline \end{array}$$

$$\begin{array}{r} 88 \\ -\ 11 \\ \hline \end{array}$$

$$\begin{array}{r} 32 \\ +\ 17 \\ \hline \end{array}$$

$$\begin{array}{r} 78 \\ -\ 22 \\ \hline \end{array}$$

$$\begin{array}{r} 45 \\ +\ 11 \\ \hline \end{array}$$

$$\begin{array}{r} 50 \\ +\ 44 \\ \hline \end{array}$$

$$\begin{array}{r} 39 \\ +\ 10 \\ \hline \end{array}$$

$$\begin{array}{r} 73 \\ -\ 40 \\ \hline \end{array}$$

$$\begin{array}{r} 13 \\ +\ 20 \\ \hline \end{array}$$

$$\begin{array}{r} 21 \\ +\ 12 \\ \hline \end{array}$$

$$\begin{array}{r} 43 \\ +\ 34 \\ \hline \end{array}$$

$$\begin{array}{r} 55 \\ -\ 22 \\ \hline \end{array}$$

$$\begin{array}{r} 67 \\ -\ 34 \\ \hline \end{array}$$

$$\begin{array}{r} 16 \\ +\ 61 \\ \hline \end{array}$$

Writing Sentences

Read each group of words. Put them in the correct order so that they form a sentence. Write the sentence on the line.

Example: bought   robot   a   him   Barry's dad

Barry's dad bought him a robot.

1.   football   The   could   play   robot

_____

2.   robot   Barry   Bruiser   his   named

_____

3.   fun   had   together   They   playing

_____

Short ŭ

Say the name of each picture.
Color the pictures that have the short sound of the vowel **u**.

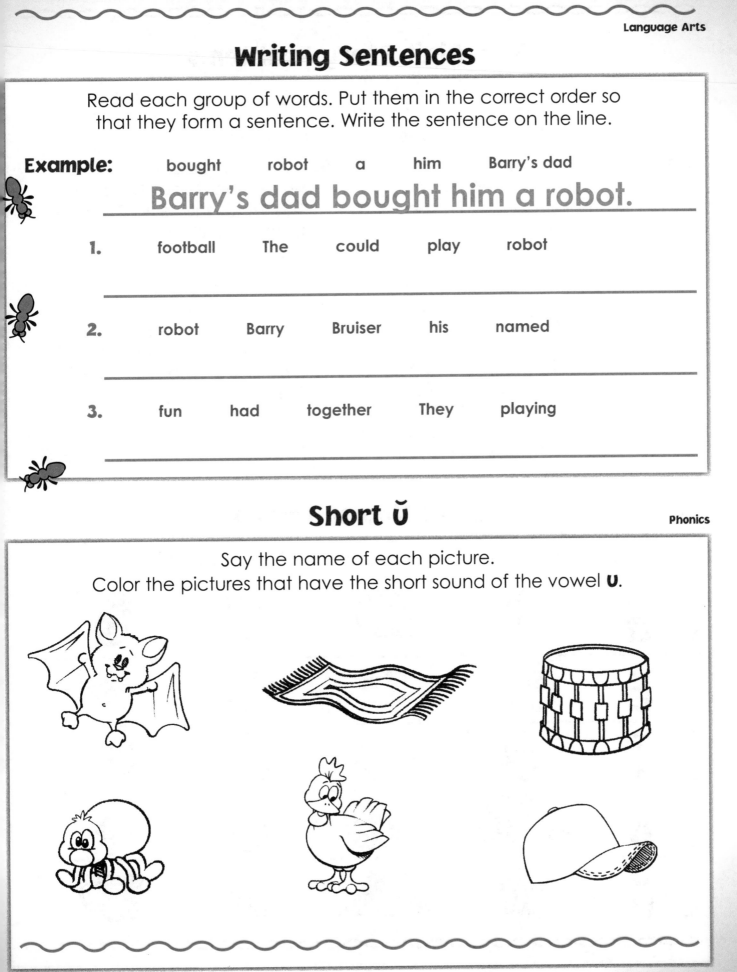

Two-Digit Story Problems

Add to solve the story problems.

A. Sam Seal had **24** balls. His trainer gave him **10** more. How many balls did Sam have altogether?

B. Susie is a great reader. Last week she read **15** books. This week she read **20**. How many books has Susie read in two weeks?

C. A monkey climbed a tree and ate **12** bananas. He threw **16** more bananas down to his friend. How many bananas were taken from the tree?

D. Tasha and Juan had a jump rope contest. Tasha jumped **56** times. Juan jumped **42** times. How many times did they jump altogether?

Short Vowel Review

Circle the picture in each row that has the short vowel sound shown.

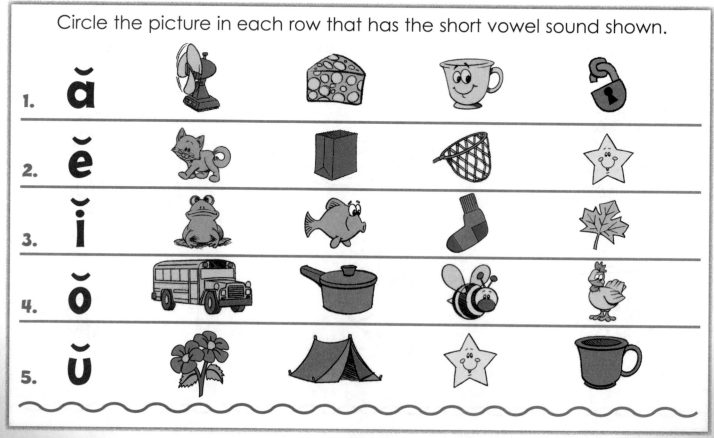

1. ă
2. ĕ
3. ĭ
4. ŏ
5. ŭ

Word Games

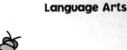

Cut apart the word cards on pages 53, 55, and 57.
Use them as flash cards, game pieces, or as described in the suggestions below.

Charades

One person or team chooses a card. That person or team then acts out the word on the card while the other players try to guess the word. Children will relax and enjoy this activity even more if it is not a competition. Create additional word cards of your own as desired.

20 Questions

Use only the noun word cards for this game. Choose one person to be "it." The person who is "it" chooses a noun card and tells whether it is a person, place, or thing. The other players ask yes or no questions to collect clues before trying to guess the noun. The object of the game is to guess the noun in fewer than 20 questions. Let a new person be "it" each time.

made	read
five	book
rode	use
light	might
chair	head

sky	my
fifty	happy
very	part
for	her
first	turn
toy	join
draw	caught
now	show

foot	glue
soon	doctor
fish	with
puzzle	supper
tiny	because
paper	seven
finish	ugly
party	magnet

Telling Time (Five-Minute Intervals)

Draw hands on the clocks to show what time it is.

A. **2:00**

B. **2:15**

C. **2:30**

D. **2:45**

E. **2:50**

F. **3:00**

Long ā

Draw an **X** on the words that do **not** have the ā sound.

bake   apple

name

race   date

ant

skate

back   tape

Color the pictures that have the ā sound.

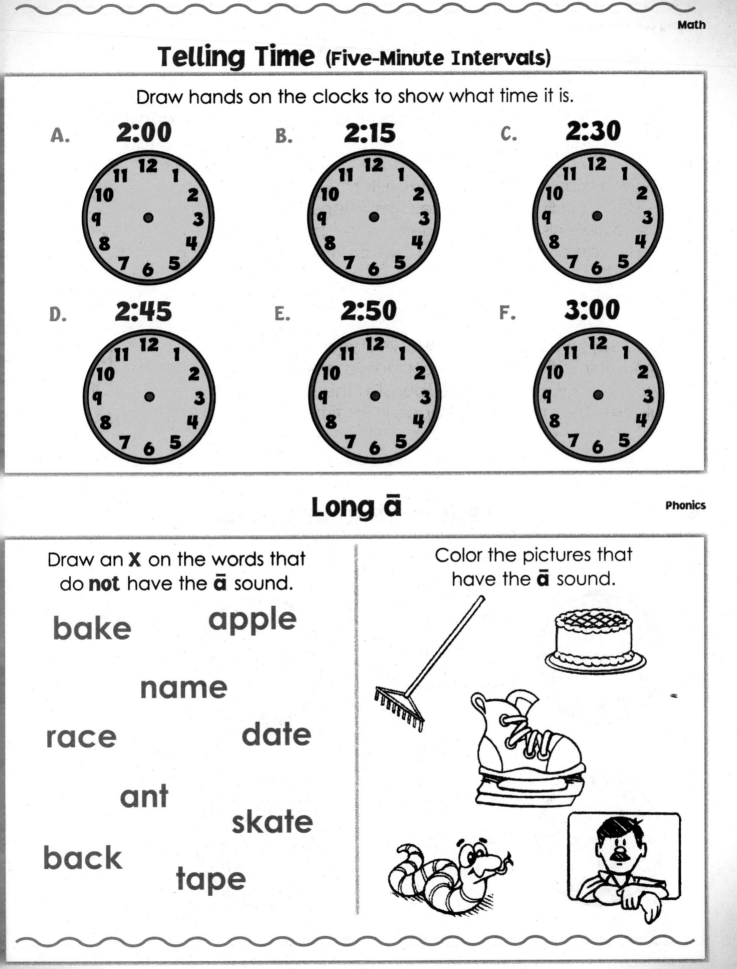

Inference

Read each poem, group of sentences, or paragraph.
Decide what each is about and circle the best answer.

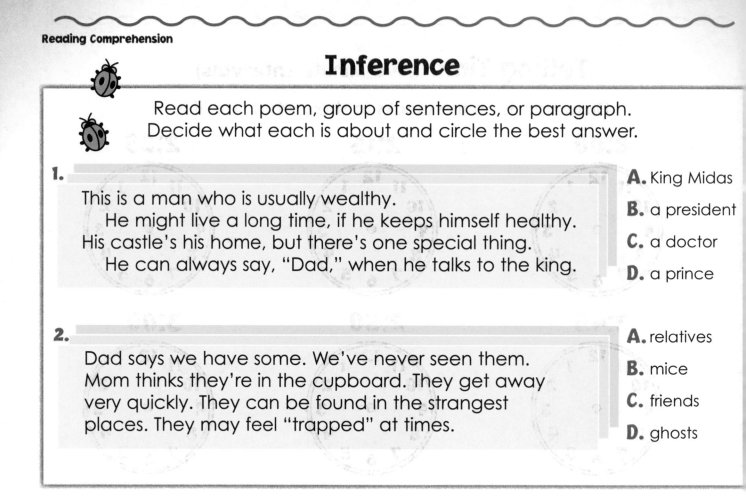

1.

This is a man who is usually wealthy.
   He might live a long time, if he keeps himself healthy.
His castle's his home, but there's one special thing.
   He can always say, "Dad," when he talks to the king.

A. King Midas

B. a president

C. a doctor

D. a prince

2.

Dad says we have some. We've never seen them.
Mom thinks they're in the cupboard. They get away
very quickly. They can be found in the strangest
places. They may feel "trapped" at times.

A. relatives

B. mice

C. friends

D. ghosts

Math

Telling Time in Words

Circle the time shown on each clock.

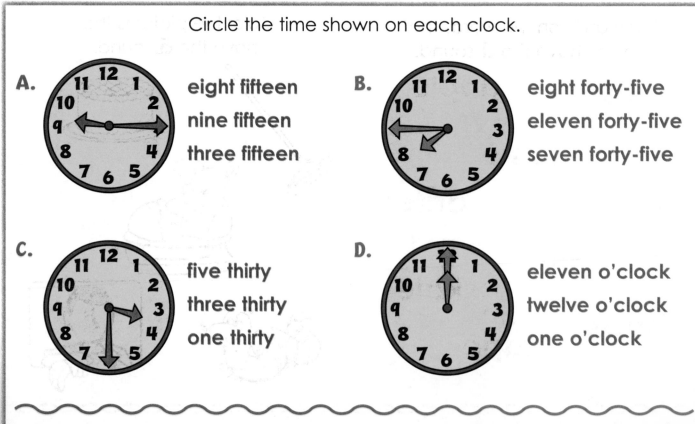

A.

eight fifteen

nine fifteen

three fifteen

B.

eight forty-five

eleven forty-five

seven forty-five

C.

five thirty

three thirty

one thirty

D.

eleven o'clock

twelve o'clock

one o'clock

Two-Digit and One-Digit Subtraction

Rewrite each number sentence in the tens and ones columns.

A. 25 − 4 = 21

tens	ones
2	5
−	4
2	1

B. 18 − 5 = 13

tens	ones
−	

C. 36 − 6 = 30

tens	ones
−	

D. 58 − 4 = 54

tens	ones
−	

Subtract to find the difference. Remember to subtract the numbers in the ones place first.

E. 22
− 1

F. 56
− 3

G. 89
− 7

H. 36
− 5

I. 63
− 2

J. 85
− 3

K. 44
− 1

L. 99
− 5

Long ē

Color the pictures that have the ē sound.

1.

Draw an **X** on the word in each row that does **not** have the ē sound.

2.   we   left   tree   see

3.   bee   eve   these   tent

Singular and Plural Possessives

Complete each phrase by writing either **'s** or **s'** on the line.

1. a monkey_____ banana

2. Kim_____ smile

3. the school_____ football team

4. the two dog_____ collars

5. the four window_____ panes

6. that book_____ cover

7. many flower_____ petals

8. the cat_____ purr

9. many monster_____ shrieks

10. several magician_____ tricks

Mixed Story Problems

Read each story problem. Use the box under
the problem to **add** or **subtract** the numbers.

Karl went surfing 38 times last summer. Steve went surfing 21 times. How many times did they go surfing altogether?

Last summer Steve lost 22 golf balls. Karl lost 20 golf balls. How many golf balls did they lose in all?

Nina and Luis jog to stay fit. Nina jogs 56 miles a week. Luis jogs 32 miles a week. How many more miles does Nina jog than Luis?

A.

B.

C.

Addition with Regrouping

To add some numbers, you must regroup.

To find the sum...	Add the ones first. $9 + 6 = 15$ 15 is **1** ten and **5** ones	Write the **5** in the ones place. Regroup the **1** into the tens place.	Add the tens. $1 + 2 = 3$	The sum is 35.
29 + 6	tens | ones 2 | 9 + | 6 ——— | 15	tens | ones 2 | 9 + | 6 ——— | 15	tens | ones ¹2 | 9 + | 6 ——— 3 | 5	¹29 + 6 ——— 35

Add to find each sum. Remember to write the number that is regrouped into the tens place. The first one has been done for you.

A. [1]
21
+ 9
———
30

B. [ ]
57
+ 5

C. [ ]
15
+ 9

D. [ ]
63
+ 7

E. [ ]
88
+ 4

R-Controlled Vowels: ar, er, or

Circle the r-controlled vowel you hear in each picture name.

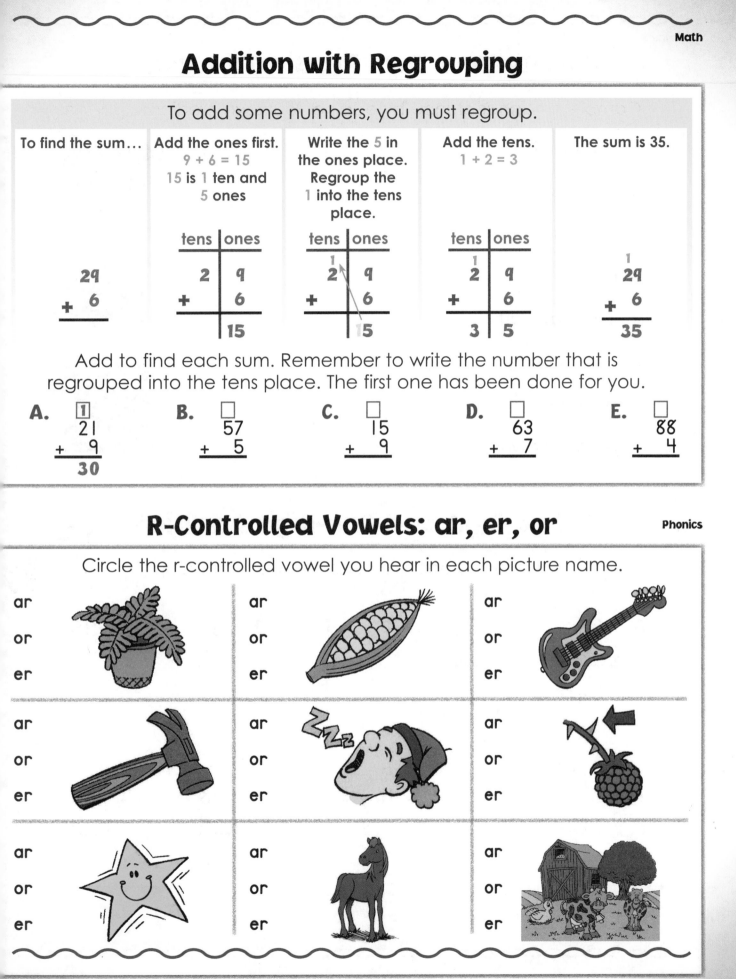

ar
or
er

ar
or
er

ar
or
er

ar
or
er

ar
or
er

ar
or
er

ar
or
er

ar
or
er

ar
or
er

Write Your Own Predicate Phrase

Complete each sentence by adding your own predicate phrase.

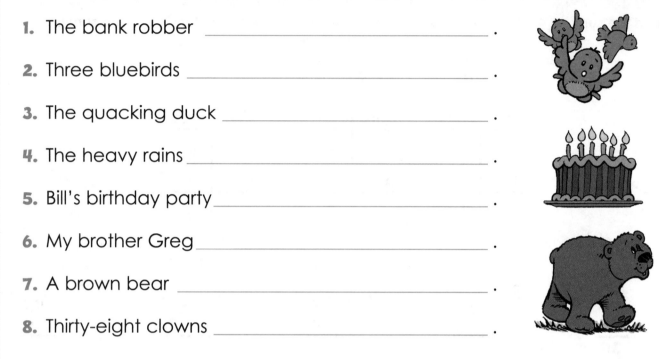

1. The bank robber _____ .

2. Three bluebirds _____ .

3. The quacking duck _____ .

4. The heavy rains _____ .

5. Bill's birthday party _____ .

6. My brother Greg _____ .

7. A brown bear _____ .

8. Thirty-eight clowns _____ .

Math

Two-Digit and One-Digit Addition

Add to find each sum. Remember to regroup.

A. 38 + 7	B. 25 + 6	C. 49 + 9	D. 34 + 6	E. 46 + 8
F. 55 + 8	G. 29 + 3	H. 71 + 9	I. 68 + 4	J. 88 + 9

Pronouns

A **pronoun** is a word that is used in place of a noun.

Kathy loves candy. $\longrightarrow$ **She loves candy.**

In this example, the noun **Kathy** can be replaced by the pronoun **she**.

Choose the correct pronoun (**he**, **she**, **it**, **we**, or **they**) to replace the highlighted word(s) in each sentence. Write the pronoun on the line.

1. **That boy** rode his bike across the lawn. _____

2. **My grandmother** tells very interesting stories. _____

3. **The bird** sat on its nest for hours. _____

4. **Carly, Fred, and I** will go to the party together. _____

5. **The roller skates** are very rusty. _____

6. **Karin** has to baby-sit tonight. _____

7. **Joelle and Betsy** went to the movies. _____

8. **The lightbulb** burned out. _____

9. **The balloons** floated up to the sky. _____

10. **Javier and I** went to the library. _____

Reading a Bar Graph

Use the **bar graph** to answer the questions.

The Number of Fish Caught

	Juan	Maria	Katie	Jordan
4				
3				
2				
1				

1. Who caught the most fish? _____

2. Who caught the fewest fish? _____

3. Who caught one fish less than Maria? _____

4. Which two children caught the same number of fish?

_____ and _____

5. How many fish did Juan and Jordan catch altogether? _____

6. Who caught one fish more than Maria? _____

7. How many fish did the children catch in all? _____

Two-Digit Addition with Regrouping

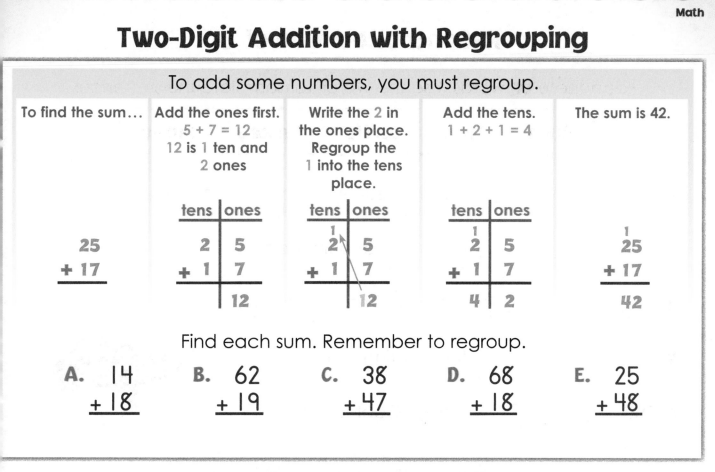

To add some numbers, you must regroup.

To find the sum…	Add the ones first. 5 + 7 = 12 12 is 1 ten and 2 ones	Write the 2 in the ones place. Regroup the 1 into the tens place.	Add the tens. 1 + 2 + 1 = 4	The sum is 42.
25 + 17	tens ones 2 5 + 1 7 ——— 12	tens ones 1 2 5 + 1 7 ——— 12	tens ones 1 2 5 + 1 7 ——— 4 2	1 25 + 17 ——— 42

Find each sum. Remember to regroup.

A. 14
+18

B. 62
+19

C. 38
+47

D. 68
+18

E. 25
+48

R-Controlled Vowel ir

Read these **ir** words. Use the words to answer the questions.

| bird | first | girl | twirl | third |

1. What is the opposite of boy? _____

2. What grade comes after second? _____

3. What do you do with a baton? _____

4. What's another word for "number one"? _____

5. What animal builds its nest in a tree? _____

R-Controlled Vowel ur

Read these **ur** words. Use the words to complete the sentences.

> **Burn**   **Turn**   **turtle**   **turkey**   **nurse**

1. A _____ is a person who helps sick people.

2. _____ means what a fire does.

3. A _____ is an animal with a shell.

4. _____ the steering wheel.

5. The _____ says, "Gobble, gobble."

Double-Digit Regrouping

Check the addition in each number sentence below. Draw a ☑ in the box if the sum is **correct**. Draw an ☒ in the box if the sum is **not correct**.

A.
```
  1
  35
+ 27
─────
  62 ☐
```

B.
```
  1
  68
+ 15
─────
  83 ☐
```

C.
```
  1
  29
+ 13
─────
  42 ☐
```

D.
```
  1
  35
+ 46
─────
  81 ☐
```

E.
```
  1
  51
+ 29
─────
  70 ☐
```

F.
```
  1
  37
+ 36
─────
  63 ☐
```

G.
```
  1
  42
+ 18
─────
  60 ☐
```

H.
```
  1
  55
+ 27
─────
  82 ☐
```

BONUS

Add together the two smallest sums from this page. What is your answer? _____

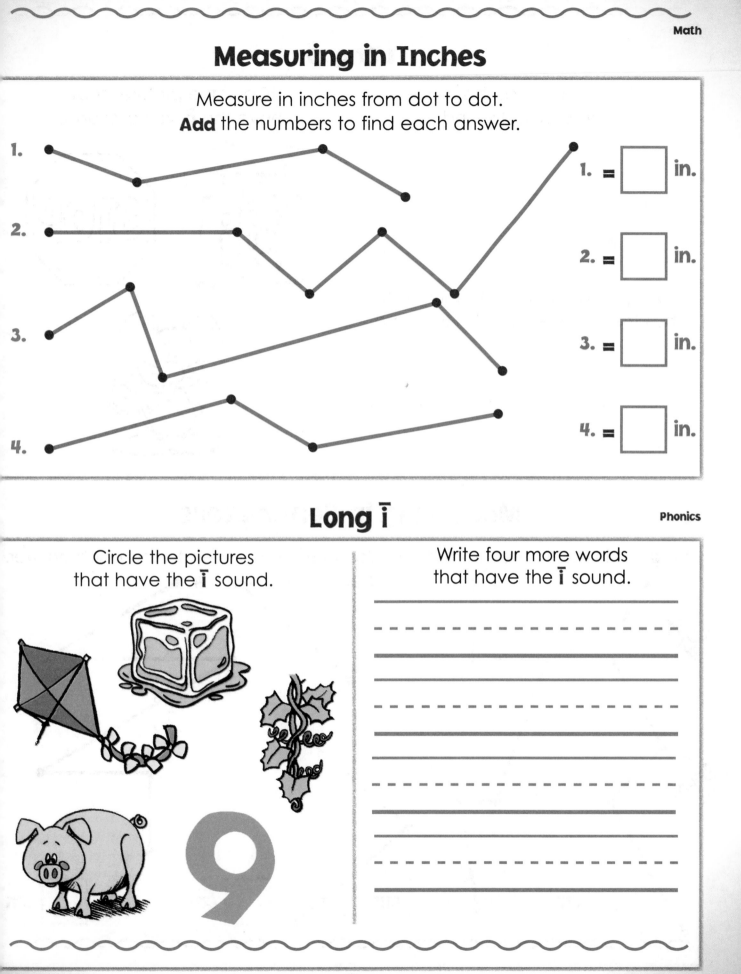

Measuring in Inches

Measure in inches from dot to dot.
Add the numbers to find each answer.

1.

2.

3.

4.

1. = ☐ in.

2. = ☐ in.

3. = ☐ in.

4. = ☐ in.

Long ī

Circle the pictures
that have the ī sound.

Write four more words
that have the ī sound.

Long ō

Circle the words that have the ō vowel sound.

nose   crop

vote   cone   joke

pop   rope

Draw a picture of something that has the ō vowel sound in its name.

Color the pictures that have the ō vowel sound.

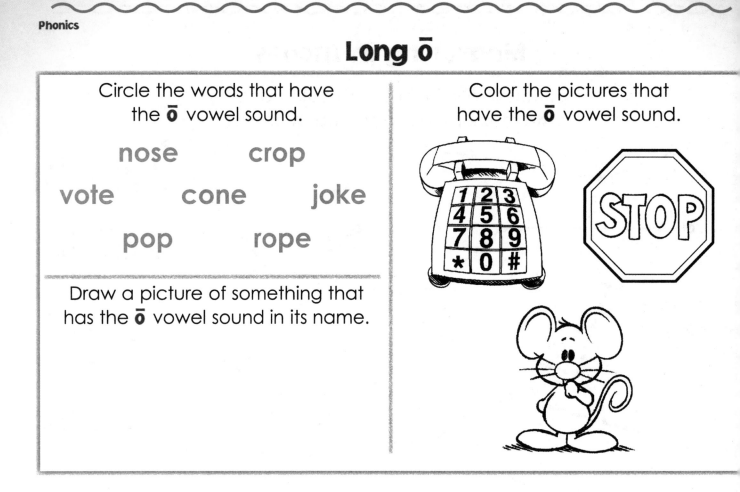

Measuring in Centimeters

Measure in centimeters from dot to dot. **Add** the numbers to find each answer.

1.   2.   3.   4.

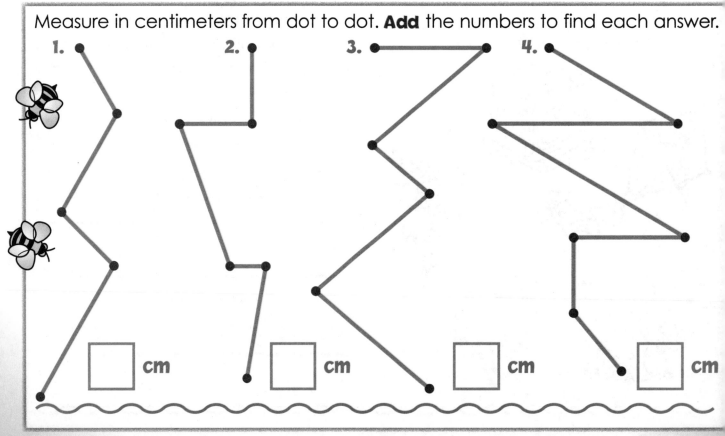

[ ] cm   [ ] cm   [ ] cm   [ ] cm

Greater Than, Less Than, or Equal To

The symbol **<** means **less than**.   12 **<** 17   (12 is less than 17)

The symbol **=** means **equal to**.   14 **=** 14   (14 is equal to 14)

The symbol **>** means **greater than**.   15 **>** 11   (15 is greater than 11)

Write the correct symbol (<, =, >) in each box to compare the numbers.

A. 16 ☐ 12

B. 17 ☐ 11

C. 15 ☐ 15

D. 13 ☐ 13

E. 15 ☐ 16

F. 13 ☐ 14

G. 18 ☐ 15

H. 19 ☐ 20

I. 17 ☐ 15

Sequencing Events

Number the sentences in each group **1–4** to show the correct order.

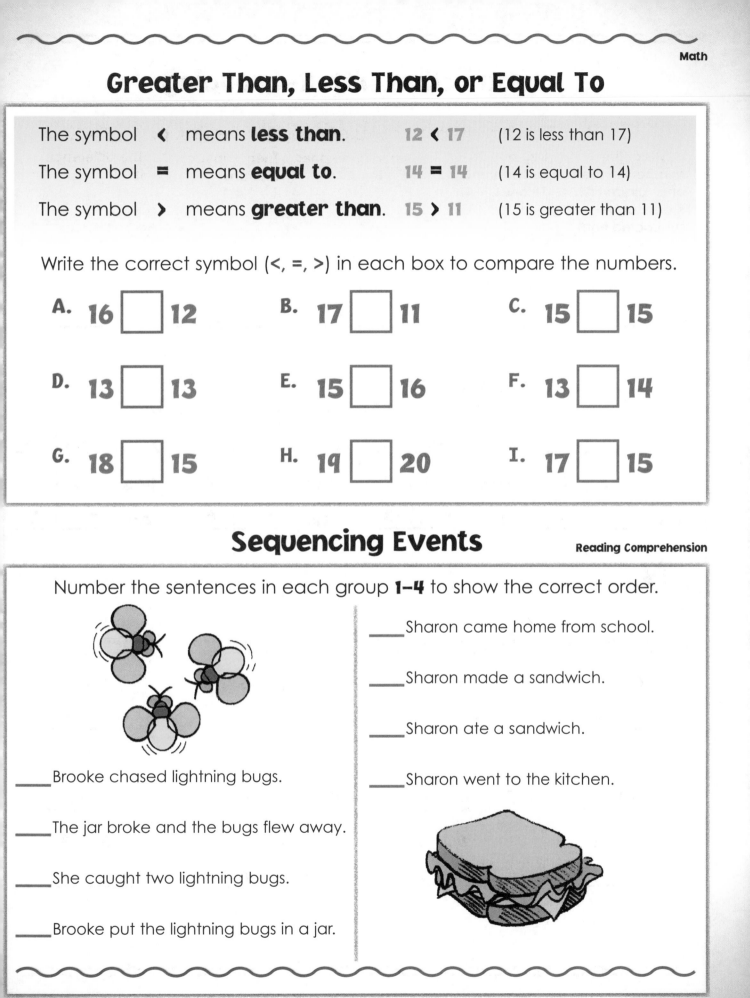

____Brooke chased lightning bugs.

____The jar broke and the bugs flew away.

____She caught two lightning bugs.

____Brooke put the lightning bugs in a jar.

____Sharon came home from school.

____Sharon made a sandwich.

____Sharon ate a sandwich.

____Sharon went to the kitchen.

Subtraction with Regrouping

To subtract some numbers, you must regroup.

Subtract the numbers in the ones place first. 8 cannot be subtracted from 5. You must regroup.	Regroup 25 as 1 ten and 15 ones.	Subtract the ones. 15 − 8 = 7	Then, subtract the tens. 1 − 0 = 1	The difference is 17.

$$\begin{array}{r} 25 \\ -\ 8 \\ \hline \end{array}$$

tens | ones
$$\begin{array}{c|c} ^1\cancel{2} & ^{15}\cancel{5} \\ - & 8 \\ \hline & \end{array}$$

tens | ones
$$\begin{array}{c|c} ^1\cancel{2} & ^{15}\cancel{5} \\ - & 8 \\ \hline & 7 \end{array}$$

tens | ones
$$\begin{array}{c|c} ^1\cancel{2} & ^{15}\cancel{5} \\ - & 8 \\ \hline 1 & 7 \end{array}$$

$$\begin{array}{r} ^1\!\!\!\!^{15}\cancel{25} \\ -\ 8 \\ \hline 17 \end{array}$$

Circle **yes** or **no** to show whether you need to regroup before subtracting. Then, subtract.

A.   yes   no
tens	ones
7	2
−	9

B.   yes   no
tens	ones
3	1
−	3

C.   yes   no
tens	ones
2	7
−	6

D.   yes   no
tens	ones
5	2
−	4

Find the difference.

E.
tens	ones
6	7
−	8

F.
tens	ones
3	3
−	2

G.
tens	ones
4	5
−	3

H.
tens	ones
3	6
−	7

I.
tens	ones
4	2
−	8

J.
tens	ones
6	1
−	7

K.
tens	ones
5	3
−	6

L.
tens	ones
3	8
−	9

Long ū

Draw an **X** on the words that do not have the **ū** sound.

fur

rule

tune

June

sun

perfume

use

flu

hug

Color the pictures that have the **ū** sound.

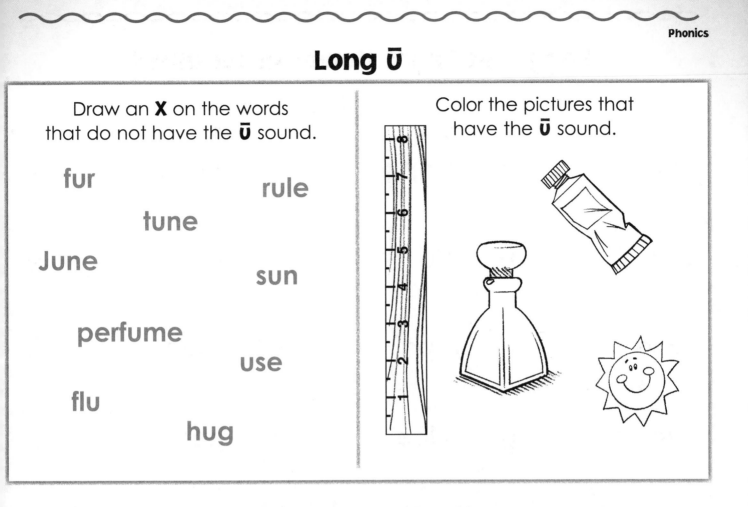

Subtract and Color

Find the difference. Color the **even** answers blue.
Color the **odd** answers red.

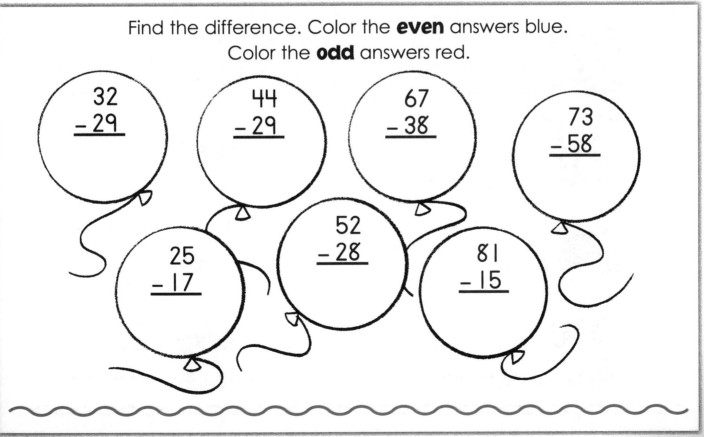

32
− 29

44
− 29

67
− 38

73
− 58

25
− 17

52
− 28

81
− 15

Long and Short Vowel Assessment

Say each word. Match the word to the correct vowel sound.

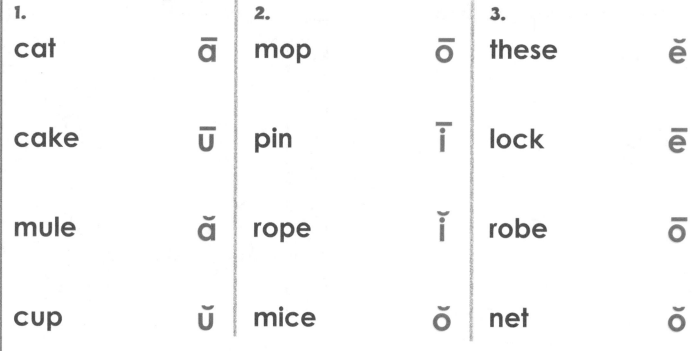

1.		2.		3.	
cat	ā	mop	ō	these	ĕ
cake	ū	pin	ī	lock	ē
mule	ă	rope	ĭ	robe	ō
cup	ŭ	mice	ŏ	net	ŏ

Say the name of each picture. Write the vowel sound you hear.
Draw the ˘ symbol or the ¯ symbol above each vowel.

4. 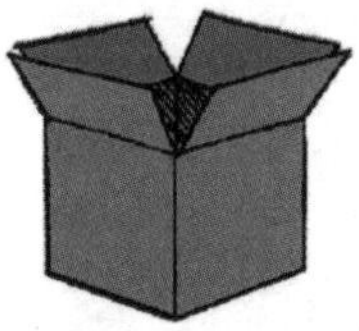

5. 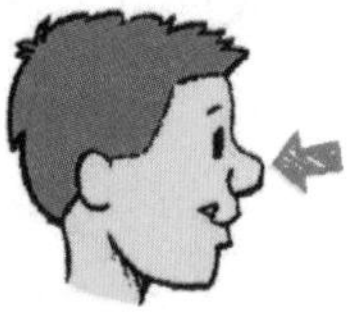

6. 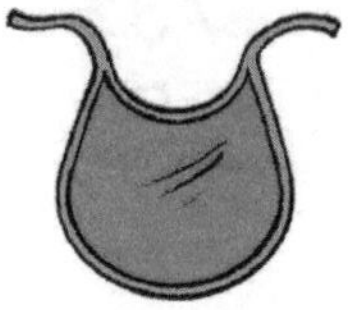

7. 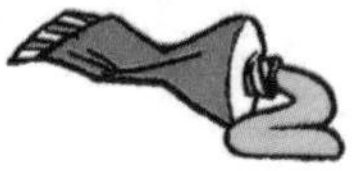

8. 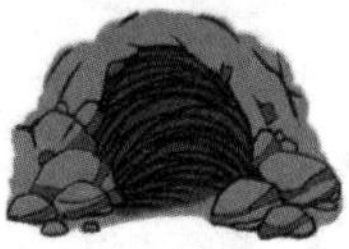

9. 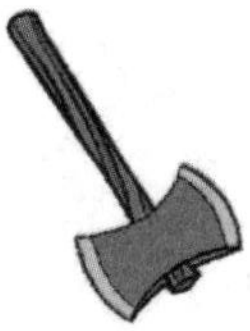

10. 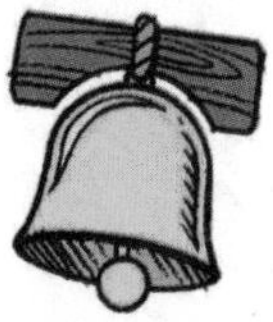

11. 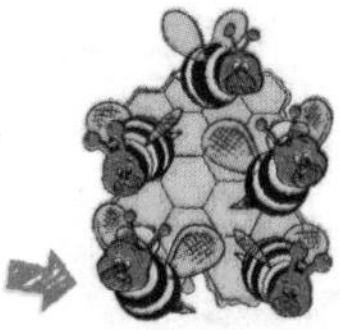

⟨, =, or ⟩

Write a number that makes each problem true. Say the problem aloud.

A. 20 ⟩ _____ **B.** 16 ⟩ _____ **C.** 12 ⟩ _____

Write a number that is equal to the first number. Say the problem aloud.

D. 13 = _____ **E.** 15 = _____ **F.** 19 = _____

Write a number that makes each problem true. Say the problem aloud.

G. 17 ⟨ _____ **H.** 11 ⟨ _____ **I.** 14 ⟨ _____

BONUS Write the number of boys in your class, then the number of girls. Write the correct symbol (<, =, >) between the numbers.

R-Controlled Vowel Review

Say the name of each picture. Circle the word that correctly names the picture. Underline **ar**, **er**, **ir**, **or**, or **ur** in each word.

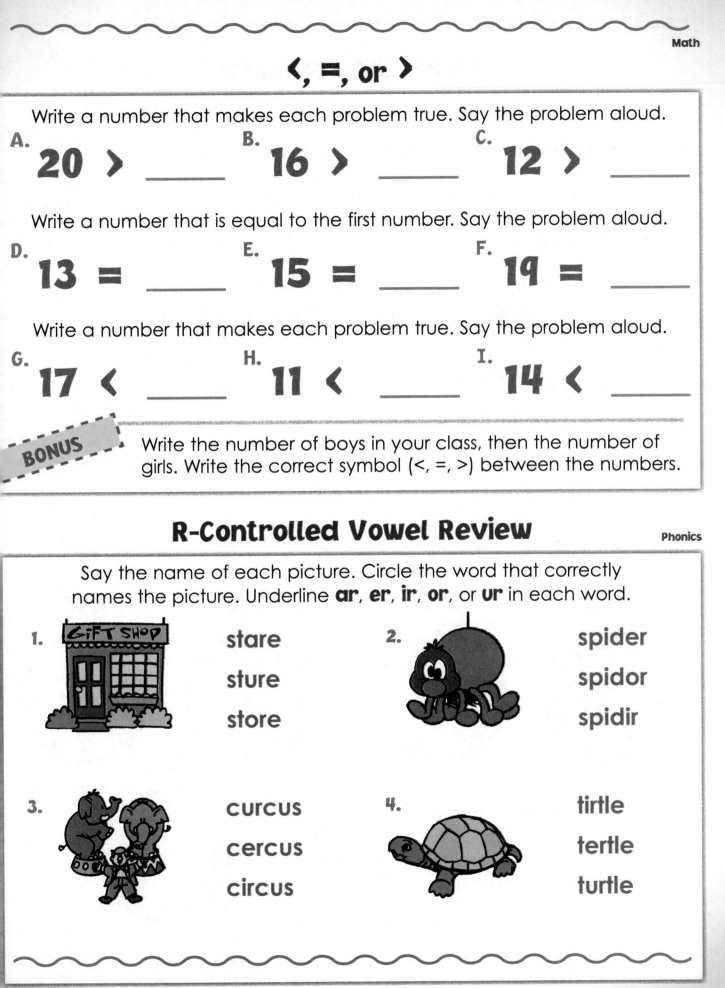

1. stare
   sture
   store

2. spider
   spidor
   spidir

3. curcus
   cercus
   circus

4. tirtle
   tertle
   turtle

Finish the Sentence

Read each sentence. Circle the correct word to complete the sentence.

1. We sat on the (**porch   purch**) and drank lemonade.

2. Karin wore a (**scerf   scarf**) around her neck.

3. The rabbit had soft, white (**fur   fer**).

Read the sentence. Write **ar**, **er**, **ir**, **or**, or **ur** to complete the word correctly in each sentence.

4. The ac_____n fell from the tree.

5. My sh_____t has stripes.

6. Meg has a new sk_____t.

7. I went to the st_____e.

Clock Problems

Draw each missing long hand.

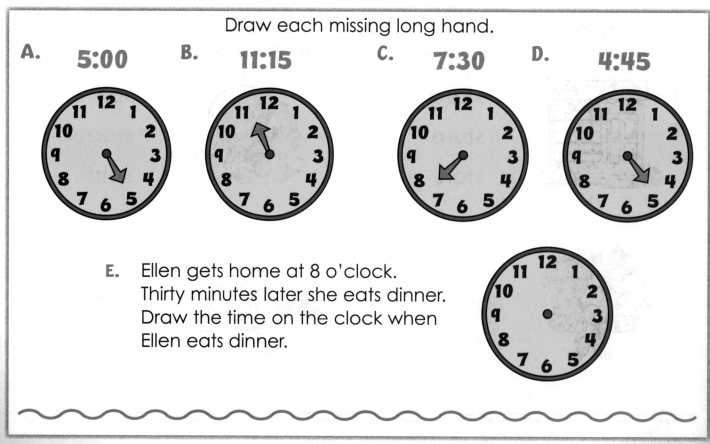

A. 5:00   B. 11:15   C. 7:30   D. 4:45

E. Ellen gets home at 8 o'clock. Thirty minutes later she eats dinner. Draw the time on the clock when Ellen eats dinner.

Identifying Coins

Color each penny. **Circle** each nickel. Draw an **X** on each dime.
Draw a **box** around each quarter. **Underline** each half-dollar.

Long and Short Vowel Review

Say each word. Color the stars with a **short vowel** sound green.
Color the stars with a **long vowel** sound purple.

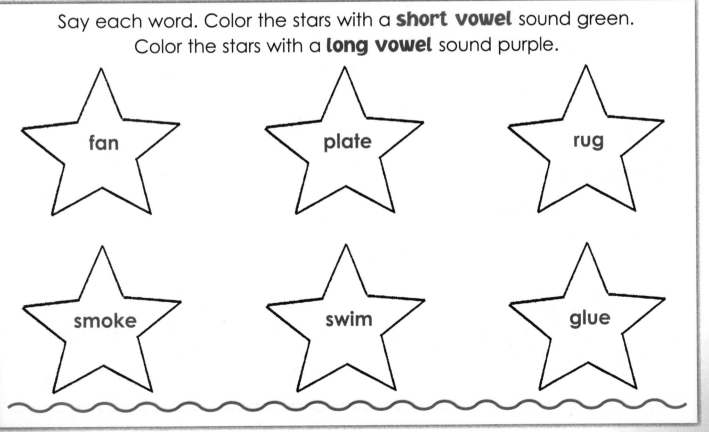

Silent e

Find the words in each row that have a long vowel sound.
Draw the ⁻ symbol above each long vowel and circle the silent **e**.

1. mile   line   lid   mice   pig

2. cut   cute   tune   huge   jug

3. case   lace   cat   sale   shape

4. pole   close   rode   cot   hole

Counting Money

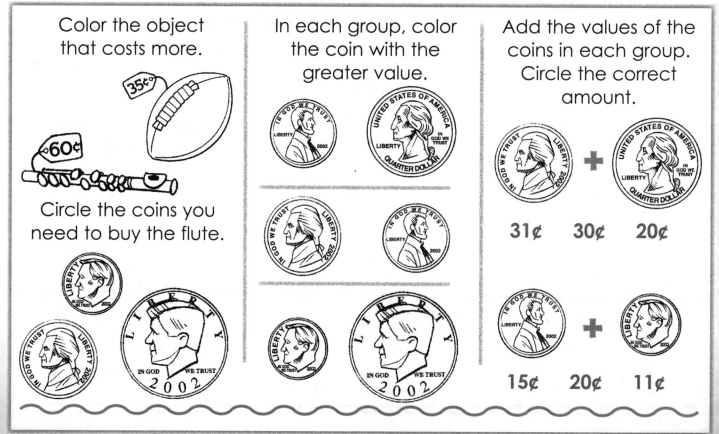

Color the object that costs more.

Circle the coins you need to buy the flute.

In each group, color the coin with the greater value.

Add the values of the coins in each group. Circle the correct amount.

31¢   30¢   20¢

15¢   20¢   11¢

Adding Coins

Write the **value** of each coin on the line below it.

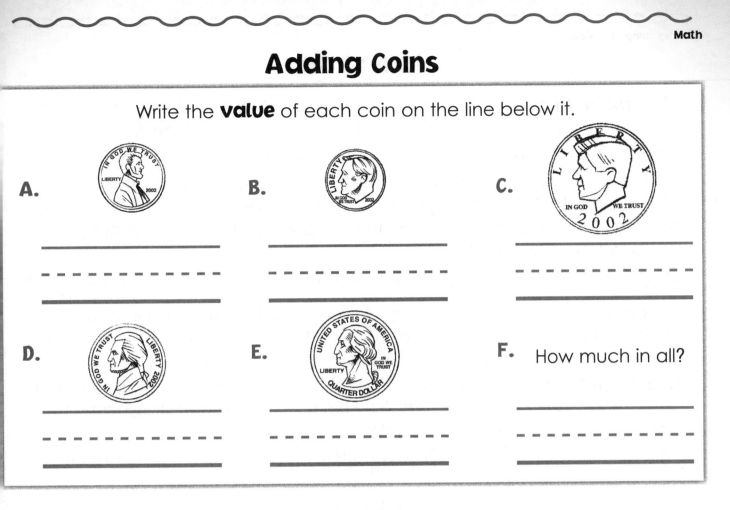

A.

B.

C.

D.

E.

F. How much in all?

Y as a Vowel

Read each word and draw a picture of it.

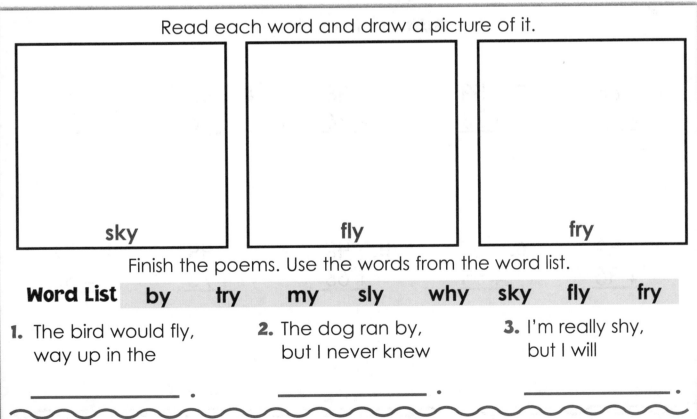

sky

fly

fry

Finish the poems. Use the words from the word list.

Word List   by   try   my   sly   why   sky   fly   fry

1. The bird would fly,
way up in the

2. The dog ran by,
but I never knew

3. I'm really shy,
but I will

_____ .   _____ .   _____ .

Main Idea

The **main idea** of a story is what the story is all about. Read each story. Underline the phrase that tells the main idea of the story.

Lisa's dog, Fletcher, knows quite a lot of tricks. They're all very nice tricks, but they are unusual. Fletcher can turn the television on by pushing the button with his nose. He turns on the garden hose with his paw when he wants a drink. Fletcher has even learned to open the mailbox. Lisa thinks that bringing in the mail is Fletcher's best trick.

A. Fletcher's unusual tricks   **B.** Lisa's dog   **C.** Fletcher gets a drink

Ryan stood looking in the bakery window for a long time. He just could not make up his mind which cake he wanted. The one with the chocolate icing looked good. Ryan also saw one that had nuts all over the top. He was ready to get that one when another cake caught his eye. There in front of him was a cake with white icing. All over the top were piled the biggest strawberries Ryan had ever seen. How would he decide?

A. The strawberry cake   **B.** Ryan's difficult decision   **C.** The bakery

Math

Addition with Regrouping

Add to find each sum.

A. 85
     + 97

B. 59
     + 78

C. 96
     + 26

D. 88
     + 76

E. 73
     + 47

F. 59
     + 96

G. 67
     + 54

H. 48
     + 68

I. 49
     + 73

J. 77
     + 86

Greater Than or Less Than

Write ‹ or › on the line for each problem.

A. 22 ____ 25   B. 13 ____ 11   C. 20 ____ 18

D. 22 ____ 38   E. 51 ____ 46   F. 67 ____ 82

G. 74 ____ 79   H. 93 ____ 65   I. 47 ____ 24

Blends: bl, br, cl, cr

Fill in the missing consonant blend: **bl**, **br**, **cl**, or **cr**.

1. ____ oom

2. ____ ock

3. ____ icket

4. ____ own

5. ____ am

6. ____ ead

7. ____ oud

8. ____ ouse

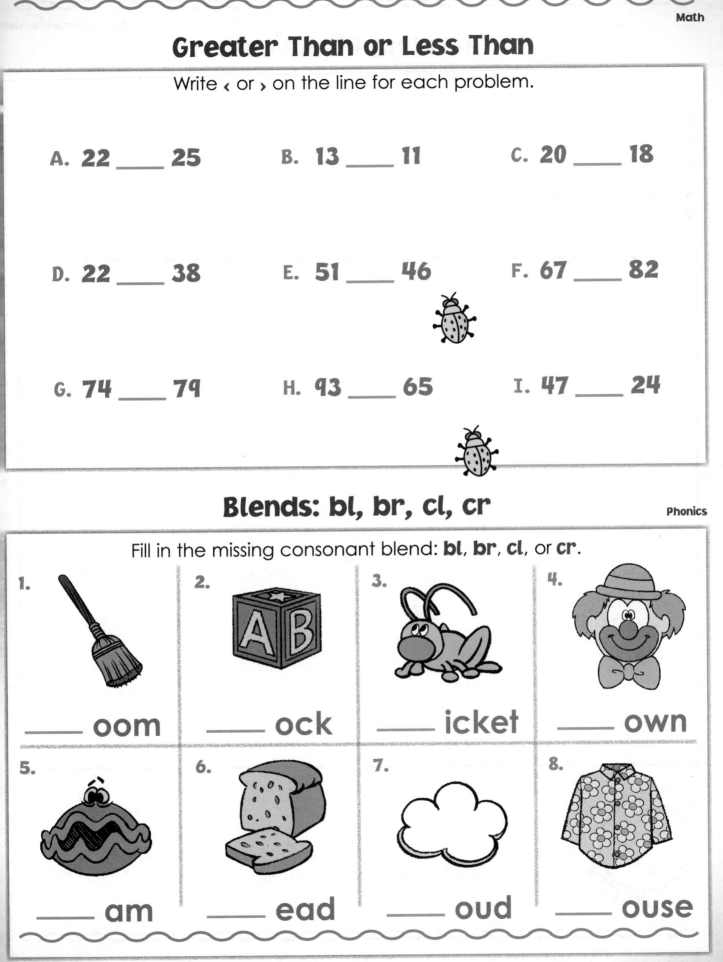

Reading Directions

Read the sentences. Follow the directions to draw the picture.

1. Draw blue water across the space.
2. Draw a green boat on the water.
3. Draw three people in the boat.
4. Draw five seagulls in the sky.
5. Draw a fishing pole at the back of the boat.
6. Draw two large fish in the water.

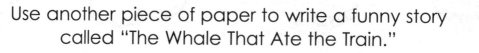

Use another piece of paper to write a funny story called "The Whale That Ate the Train."

Dollar Bill

Look at the money below. Underline the best word in each sentence.

A. This is a dollar (bill   coin).

B. It is worth (10   100) cents.

C. This is equal to (one   five) dollar(s).

D. One way to write this amount is ($1.00 $10.0).

BRAIN BUILDER

How many pennies in a dollar?	How many nickels in a dollar?	How many dimes in a dollar?	How many quarters in a dollar?	How many dollars in a dollar?

Blends: dr, fl, fr

Fill in the missing consonant blend: **dr**, **fl**, or **fr**.

1. ☐ ap

2. ☐ aft

3. ☐ ost

4. ☐ ash

5. ☐ eeze

6. ☐ ink

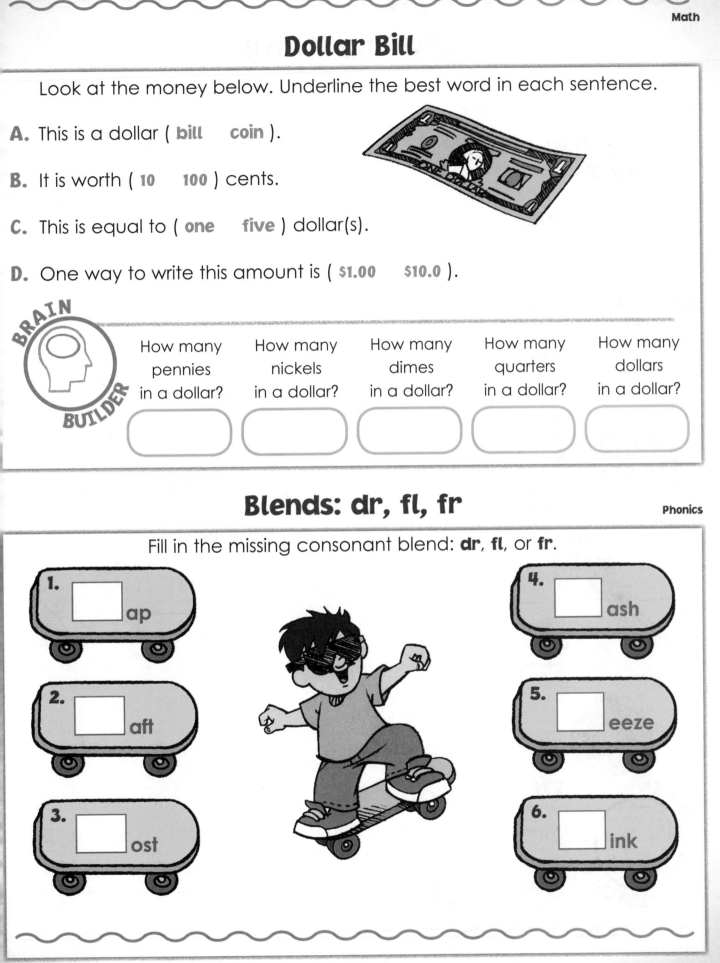

Counting Money

Color the exact coins you need to buy each item.

A. pack of gum

42¢

B. taffy

37¢

C. lemon drops

66¢

D. lollipop

93¢

E. fireball

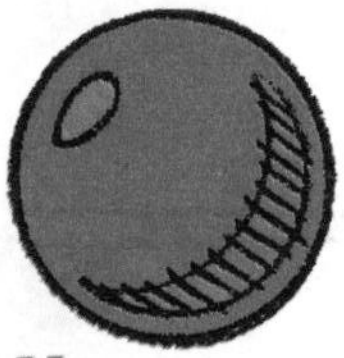

17¢

BRAIN BUILDER

What two kinds of candy could you buy with exactly $1.03?

_____ and _____

Blends: gl, gr, pl, pr

Fill in the missing consonant blend: **gl**, **gr**, **pl**, or **pr**.

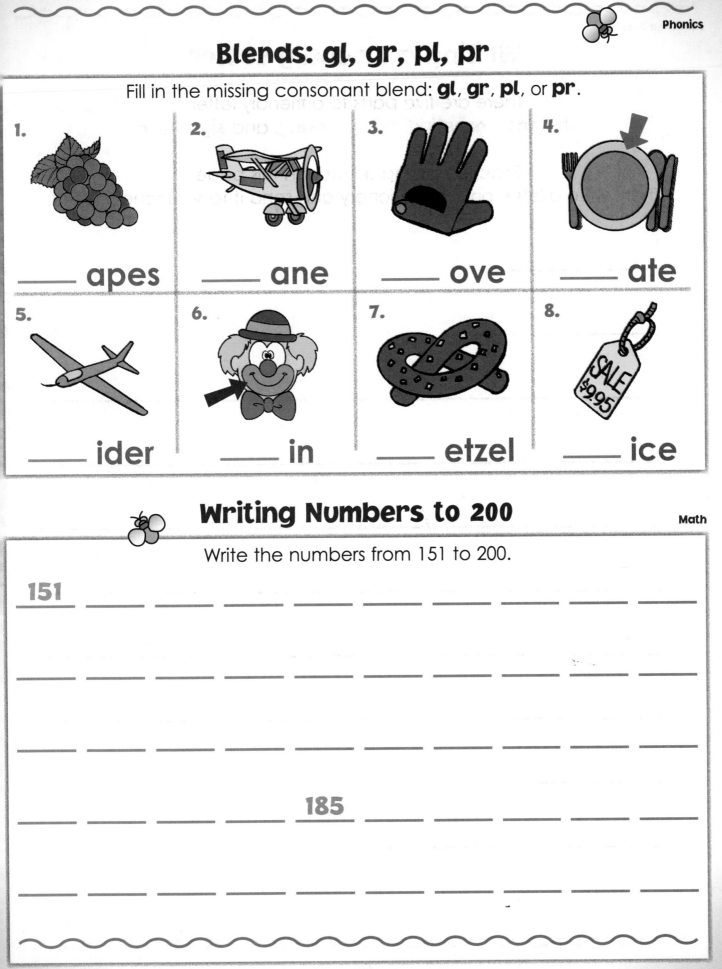

1. _____ apes

2. _____ ane

3. _____ ove

4. _____ ate

5. _____ ider

6. _____ in

7. _____ etzel

8. _____ ice

Writing Numbers to 200

Write the numbers from 151 to 200.

151 _____ _____ _____ _____ _____ _____ _____ _____

_____ _____ _____ _____ _____ _____ _____ _____ _____

_____ _____ _____ _____ _____ _____ _____ _____ _____

_____ _____ _____ _____ 185 _____ _____ _____ _____ _____

_____ _____ _____ _____ _____ _____ _____ _____ _____

Writing a Friendly Letter

There are five parts to a friendly letter:
the **date**, **greeting**, **body**, **closing**, and **signature**.

Practice writing a letter on this page.
Then, write a letter on real stationery and send it to someone special.

_____
(date)

_____
(greeting)

_____
(body of letter)

_____

_____

_____

_____

_____

_____,
(closing)

_____
(signature)

Mixed Problems

Write **<**, **>**, or **=** in the circle.

8
16 − 8 **=** 14 − 6   6 + 7 ◯ 4 + 3   8 + 5 ◯ 7 + 6

6 + 9 ◯ 7 + 8   5 + 8 ◯ 6 + 8   17 − 9 ◯ 18 − 9

17 − 8 ◯ 3 + 7   7 + 8 ◯ 8 + 7   5 + 2 ◯ 15 − 7

15 − 5 ◯ 6 + 4   6 + 4 ◯ 12 − 2   9 + 3 ◯ 6 + 8

Blends: sk, sl, sm, sn

Fill in the missing consonant blend: **sk**, **sl**, **sm**, or **sn**.

1. ____ ate

2. ____ ile

3. ____ ake

4. ____ ed

5. ____ oke

6. ____ ull

7. ____ eeve

8. ____ eakers

A Dinosaur Story

Read the paragraph below.

Millions of years ago, dinosaurs lived on Earth. The word "dinosaur" means "terrible lizard." Some dinosaurs were 30 times bigger than an elephant. Many dinosaurs ate plants, but some ate meat. Dinosaurs became extinct, or died out, a long time ago.

Answer the questions about the paragraph you just read. Use complete sentences.

1. What does the word "dinosaur" mean?

_____

2. When did dinosaurs live on Earth?

_____

3. Did all dinosaurs eat plants?

_____

4. How big were some dinosaurs?

_____

5. Are there dinosaurs on Earth now?

_____

6. What does "extinct" mean?

_____

BRAIN BUILDER

What kind of meat do you think some dinosaurs ate?

_____

Fractions: ½, ⅓, ¼

Draw lines to divide each shape into fractions. Color each fraction.

A. ½

B. ¼

C. ⅓

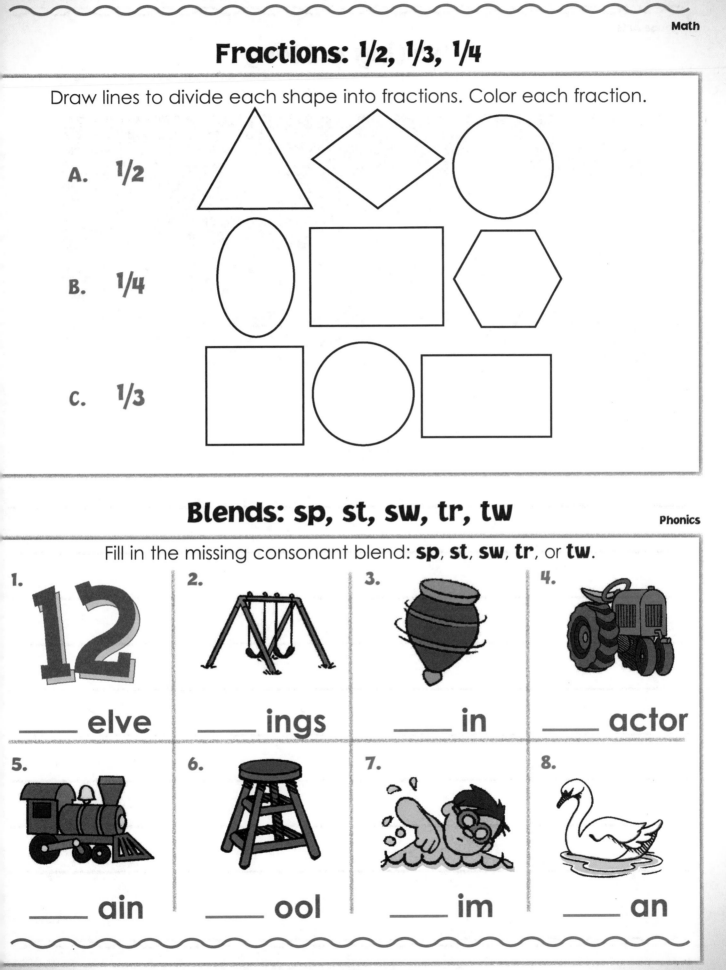

Blends: sp, st, sw, tr, tw

Fill in the missing consonant blend: **sp**, **st**, **sw**, **tr**, or **tw**.

1. ___ elve

2. ___ ings

3. ___ in

4. ___ actor

5. ___ ain

6. ___ ool

7. ___ im

8. ___ an

Writing a Story

Pretend you are taking a trip to the moon.
Use complete sentences to list eight or more things you will do there.

_____

_____

_____

_____

_____

_____

_____

_____

Double-Digit Addition

Add to find the sum.

A.	hundreds	tens	ones
		3	8
+		7	4

B.	hundreds	tens	ones
		5	9
+		8	3

C.	hundreds	tens	ones
		7	5
+		6	1

D. 66
  + 72

E. 89
  + 62

F. 63
  + 51

G. 78
  + 54

H. 96
  + 95

Consonant Blend Review

Read each sentence. Underline the word that best completes each sentence. Circle the blend.

1. The _____ are having a birthday party.   plants   grounds   twins

2. I need scissors and _____ for art class.   glue   small   ski

3. I like to _____ in front of people.   speak   plus   slope

4. The _____ at the circus was funny.   slim   stars   clown

5. The baby's skin felt very _____ .   smooth   clam   brain

6. I picked a _____ for my mother.   snail   flower   sport

7. Water helps plants _____ .   grow   twist   spot

Regrouping with Story Problems

In story problems, phrases like **take away** and
how many are left tell you to subtract.

Sherri had **24** raisins.
She ate **16** of the raisins.
How many raisins were left?

$$\begin{array}{r} \overset{1\ 14}{2\,4} \\ -\ 1\ 6 \\ \hline 8 \end{array}$$

Sherri had **8**
raisins left.

Show your work in the box for each story problem.
Circle the clue phrases that tell you to subtract.

A.
The pet shop had
25 kittens for sale.
19 kittens were sold.
How many kittens
were left at the
pet store?

B.
Mark had **51** nails.
He used **27** nails to
build a birdhouse.
How many nails
were left?

C.
The toy box had
20 toys in it. The
teacher let the
children take out
7 toys. How many
toys were left in
the toy box?

D.
Bobo the clown
had **42** balloons.
Bobo gave **24**
balloons to the
children. How
many balloons did
Bobo have left?

Write a story problem for the number sentence. Then, write the difference.

E. $\begin{array}{r} 71 \\ -59 \\ \hline \end{array}$ _____

_____

Consonant Blend Assessment

Circle the beginning blend in each word.

1. block	2. grape	3. skunk	4. drum	5. glue
6. sled	7. crown	8. smile	9. star	10. snail
11. frame	12. clown	13. swing	14. spider	15. twig
16. plant	17. crush	18. train	19. flower	20. pretzel

Say the name of each picture.
Circle the blend you hear at the beginning of the word.

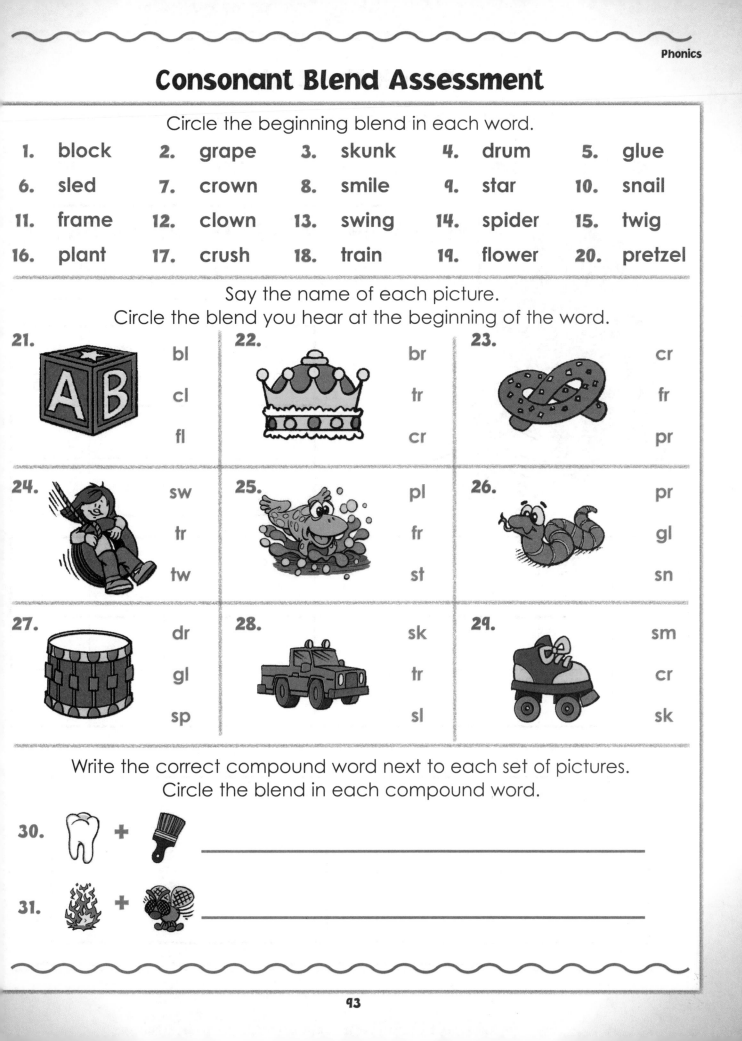

21. bl   cl   fl

22. br   tr   cr

23. cr   fr   pr

24. sw   tr   tw

25. pl   fr   st

26. pr   gl   sn

27. dr   gl   sp

28. sk   tr   sl

29. sm   cr   sk

Write the correct compound word next to each set of pictures.
Circle the blend in each compound word.

30. _____

31. _____

Break the Code

Subtract. Remember to regroup. Use the code to solve the riddle.

What did dinosaurs have that no other animal has ever had?

46	25	64	37	47	19	49	28	58	17
D	B	N	A	R	U	S	Y	O	I

53 − 28	71 − 34	84 − 59	46 − 18

63 − 17	75 − 58	92 − 28	84 − 26	63 − 14	96 − 59	37 − 18	66 − 19	65 − 16

Rewrite in column form. Regroup and subtract.

A. 83 − 68 =

B. 44 − 27 =

Regrouping with Three Addends

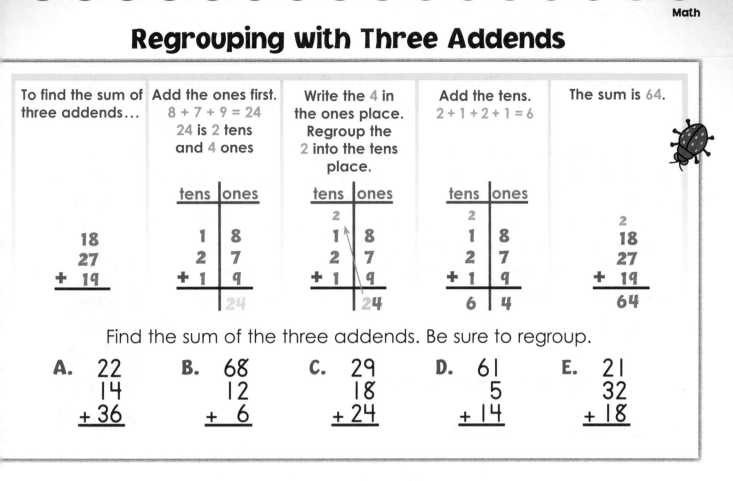

Find the sum of the three addends. Be sure to regroup.

A. 22
    14
    + 36

B. 68
    12
    + 6

C. 29
    18
    + 24

D. 61
    5
    + 14

E. 21
    32
    + 18

Descriptive Sentences

A **descriptive sentence** tells details about something.

The loud, black dog barked at the pretty woman.

Write a descriptive sentence about each topic below.

1. a white cloud

_____

2. a sad giraffe

_____

3. a yellow taxi

_____

4. the small mouse

_____

Main Idea

Read each story. Choose the phrase that tells the main idea of the story. Write the letter of the correct phrase in the box.

For a monkey, Cici wasn't doing badly at all. Still, the zookeeper thought she should learn some new tricks. Cici was sent to gymnastics classes. So far, Cici has learned to swing from the rings quite well, and she can almost walk across the balance beam. Cici's teacher wants her to learn to do some stunts on the trampoline, too. Cici thinks that swinging, bouncing, and jumping were all easier in the jungle!

A. Cici takes gymnastic lessons

B. A monkey with a good home

C. Cici and the zookeeper

Math

Regrouping with Three Addends

Find the sums. Remember to regroup.

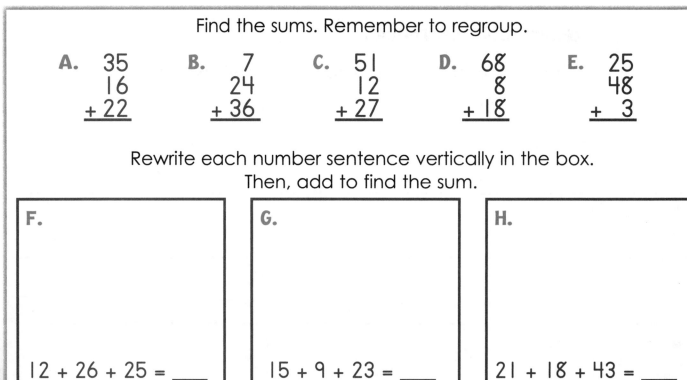

A.	**B.**	**C.**	**D.**	**E.**
35	7	51	68	25
16	24	12	8	48
+ 22	+ 36	+ 27	+ 18	+ 3

Rewrite each number sentence vertically in the box.
Then, add to find the sum.

F.

12 + 26 + 25 = ____

G.

15 + 9 + 23 = ____

H.

21 + 18 + 43 = ___

Consonant Digraphs: ch, sh, th

Read the words in the word list. Write each word below its beginning digraph.

Word List

chip	shy	thumb
thin	chin	ship
thick	sheep	chunk

1. **ch**

2. **sh**

3. **th**

Writing Descriptive Sentences

1. Write a descriptive sentence about something in your house.

2. Write a descriptive sentence about a friend.

3. Write a descriptive sentence about an animal.

Quotation Marks

Quotation marks (" ") are placed around
words people say in a sentence.

Mr. Ving said, "Good morning, class."

In each sentence, underline the exact words spoken by the person.
Put quotation marks around the quotation.

1. Frank said to Paula, I enjoyed playing with you today.

2. I hope I can go to the party, said Derek.

3. This pizza is delicious! exclaimed Chris.

4. William saw the ice cream and said to his mom, May I have some, please?

Consonant Digraphs: ch, sh, th

Say the name of each picture. Circle its beginning sound.

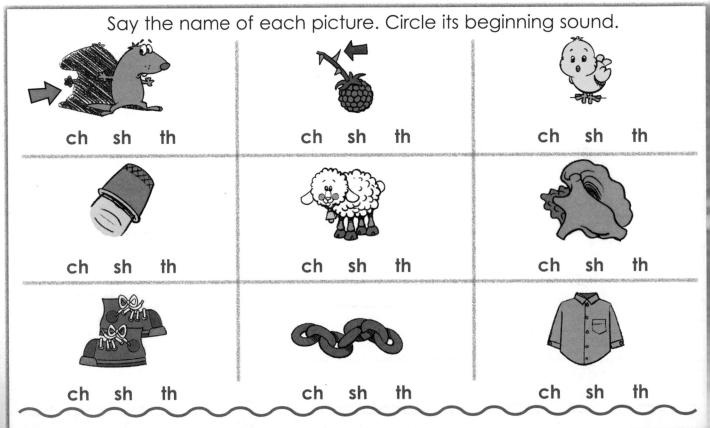

ch   sh   th   ch   sh   th   ch   sh   th

ch   sh   th   ch   sh   th   ch   sh   th

ch   sh   th   ch   sh   th   ch   sh   th

Finish the Patterns

Draw lines to continue each pattern.

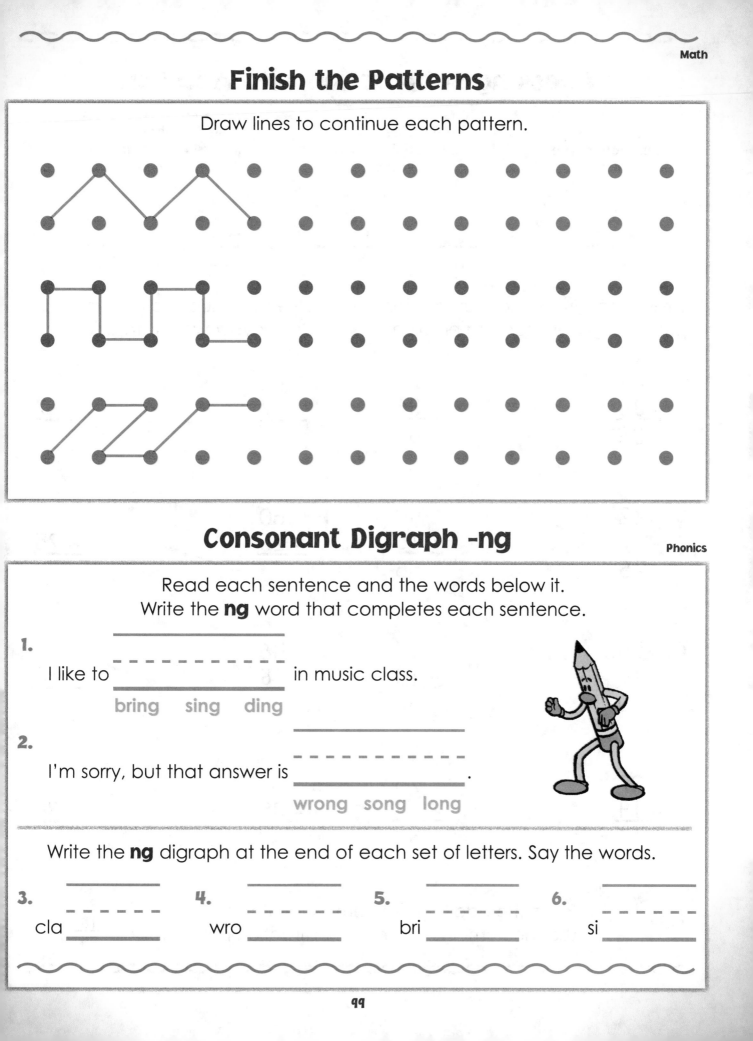

Consonant Digraph -ng

Read each sentence and the words below it.
Write the **ng** word that completes each sentence.

1.

I like to _____ in music class.

bring   sing   ding

2.

I'm sorry, but that answer is _____ .

wrong   song   long

Write the **ng** digraph at the end of each set of letters. Say the words.

3. cla _____

4. wro _____

5. bri _____

6. si _____

Checking Subtraction with Addition

To check subtraction with addition . . .	Add the difference to the amount that was subtracted.	This sum should equal the first number from the subtraction sentence.

$$\begin{array}{r} 65 \\ -\ 27 \\ \hline 38 \end{array}$$

$$\begin{array}{r} \overset{5\ 15}{\cancel{65}} \\ -\ 27 \\ \hline 38 \end{array} \qquad \begin{array}{r} 38 \\ +\ 27 \\ \hline \end{array}$$

$$\begin{array}{r} \overset{5\ 15}{\cancel{65}} \\ -\ 27 \\ \hline 38 \end{array} \qquad \begin{array}{r} 38 \\ +\ 27 \\ \hline 65 \end{array}$$

Draw a line from each subtraction problem to the checking problem.

A. $\begin{array}{r} 62 \\ -\ 36 \\ \hline 26 \end{array}$ $\qquad$ $\begin{array}{r} 26 \\ +\ 36 \\ \hline 62 \end{array}$

B. $\begin{array}{r} 82 \\ -\ 7 \\ \hline 75 \end{array}$ $\qquad$ $\begin{array}{r} 40 \\ +\ 16 \\ \hline 56 \end{array}$

C. $\begin{array}{r} 56 \\ -\ 16 \\ \hline 40 \end{array}$ $\qquad$ $\begin{array}{r} 18 \\ +\ 19 \\ \hline 37 \end{array}$

D. $\begin{array}{r} 37 \\ -\ 19 \\ \hline 18 \end{array}$ $\qquad$ $\begin{array}{r} 75 \\ +\ 7 \\ \hline 82 \end{array}$

Solve each subtraction problem. Check your work with addition.

E. $\begin{array}{r} 83 \\ -\ 17 \\ \hline \end{array}$ $\qquad$ $\begin{array}{r} \\ +\ 17 \\ \hline \end{array}$

F. $\begin{array}{r} 50 \\ -\ 25 \\ \hline \end{array}$ $\qquad$ $\begin{array}{r} \\ +\ 25 \\ \hline \end{array}$

G. $\begin{array}{r} 46 \\ -\ 18 \\ \hline \end{array}$ $\qquad$ $\begin{array}{r} \\ +\ 18 \\ \hline \end{array}$

H. $\begin{array}{r} 57 \\ -\ 38 \\ \hline \end{array}$ $\qquad$ $\begin{array}{r} \\ +\ 38 \\ \hline \end{array}$

BONUS

Read the addition problem to the right.
Use the numbers to write a subtraction problem.

$$\begin{array}{r} 36 \\ +\ 18 \\ \hline 54 \end{array}$$

Hundred Chart

Write the numbers to complete the hundred chart.

1			4		6	7			
	12			15			18		
21			24		26				30
		33				37		39	
	42				46		48		
51			54			57			60
		63		65				69	
71			74		76				80
		83					88		
91			94			97			100

Time yourself. How fast can you count to 100?

A High-Flying Story

This baby eagle needs help. Read the story to learn more about it.

A High Flyer

Deke is a baby bald eagle who is learning to fly. It has been a real **hardship** for Deke. He has been practicing for days. He just does not seem to be **improving**.

Getting up in the air was easy. Flying over the plains was no problem. But Deke has trouble flying around things. He does not do well when he **attempts** to land on a certain spot, either. It is hard for Deke to face his friends. Perhaps he should sign up for flying lessons to better his flying skills.

Write the letter of the best answer on each line.

____ 1. The word **hardship** means:
   a. something that is not easy
   b. a boat
   c. a broken wing
   d. stony

____ 2. The word **improving** means:
   a. getting better
   b. feeling sad
   c. feeling sore
   d. getting lost

____ 3. A word in the story that means the opposite of **hairy** is:
   a. problem
   b. practicing
   c. around
   d. bald

____ 4. In the story, the word **He** stands for:
   a. Deke's friend
   b. Deke
   c. Deke's dad
   d. the teacher

____ 5. A word in the story that means almost the same as **maybe** is:
   a. perhaps
   b. certain
   c. probably
   d. problem

____ 6. The word **attempts** means:
   a. sings
   b. tries
   c. waits
   d. laughs

Writing Fractions

Write the fraction of shaded parts shown in each set.

A. $\dfrac{1}{2}$

B. ____

C. ____

D. ____

E. ____

F. ____

Hard and Soft c

Circle either **k** or **s** to show whether the word has the
hard c sound (as in cloud) or the **soft c** sound (as in city).

1. comb
k   s

2. cape
k   s

3. celery
k   s

4. lettuce
k   s

5. welcome
k   s

6. cellar
k   s

7. certain
k   s

8. terrific
k   s

9. princess
k   s

10. police
k   s

11. office
k   s

12. overcoat
k   s

13. popcorn
k   s

14. volcano
k   s

Hard and Soft g

Circle either **g** or **j** to show whether the word has the
hard g sound (as in gum) or the **soft g** sound (as in gem).

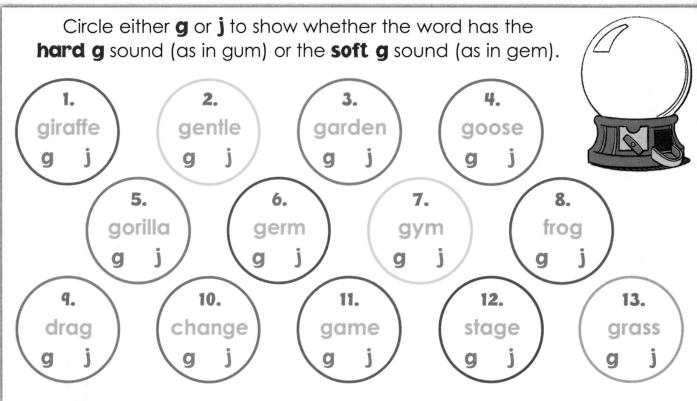

1. giraffe
g   j

2. gentle
g   j

3. garden
g   j

4. goose
g   j

5. gorilla
g   j

6. germ
g   j

7. gym
g   j

8. frog
g   j

9. drag
g   j

10. change
g   j

11. game
g   j

12. stage
g   j

13. grass
g   j

More Fractions

Fill in the boxes to name each fraction.

	Part Shaded	Parts in All	Fraction
A.			
B.			

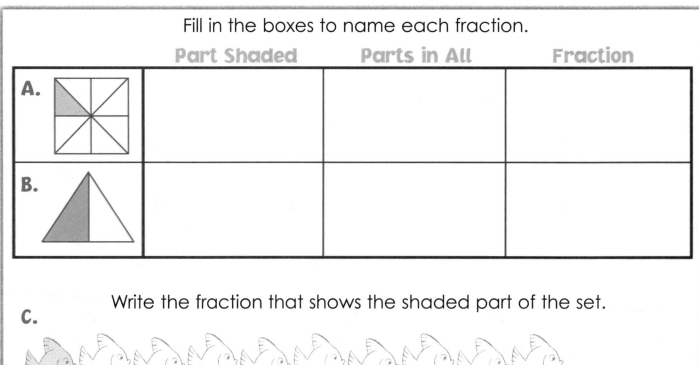

Write the fraction that shows the shaded part of the set.

C.

_____

Hard and Soft c and g

Cut and paste each picture under the correct beginning sound.

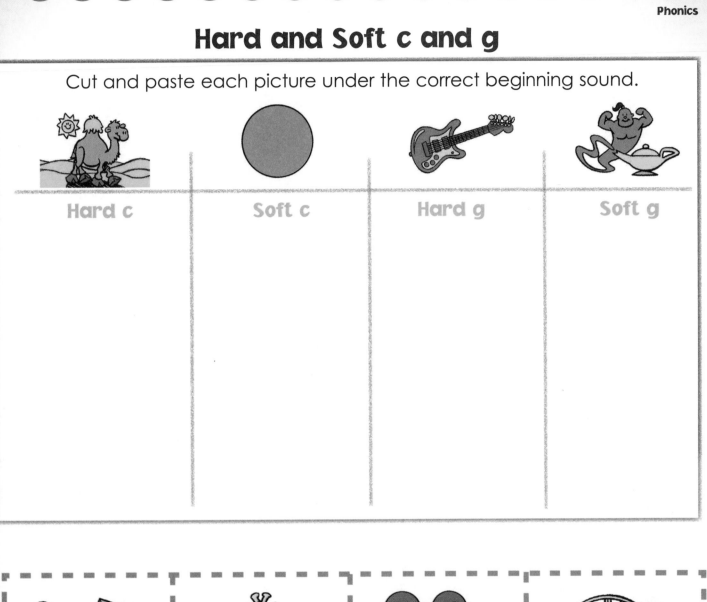

Hard c	Soft c	Hard g	Soft g

Paul Bunyan and Babe the Blue Ox

Paul Bunyan was the greatest lumberjack of all time. People still talk about him, even today. He was the biggest, strongest, and smartest logger in the whole world.

1

When little Paul started to crawl, he caused earthquakes. People in town began to complain. Paul's parents soon built him a cradle and set it just off the coast near their house. The waves soothed Paul and rocked him to sleep. But when he moved around, he caused tidal waves.

3

Nobody knows for sure, but most say Paul was born in Maine. He weighed well over 50 pounds at birth. It took a whole herd of cows to make enough milk to feed him. Amazed, Paul's parents watched their son grow three feet taller each day.

2

As Paul grew bigger, it was harder and harder for his parents to care for him. Paul's parents knew they had to do something. One day, they took Paul to a place in the middle of the woods. They gave him some simple tools, a fishing pole, and an axe. Then, they said good-bye.

4

Paul cried for days and days. When he finally stopped, he saw that his tears had formed a river. He used his fishing pole to catch some fish and had a great big meal. After that, he began to feel better.

One day, as he walked through the snow, Paul saw a pair of ears sticking out of a snowdrift. He thought he heard a muffled cry. It sounded like "Mama." When Paul brushed away the snow, he found a frozen baby ox. It had turned blue from the cold. Paul held the ox in his arms and took him back to his home. There he built a big fire and sat with the ox until it warmed up.

Soon he was chopping down trees for firewood and hunting and fishing for every meal. Paul was a natural woodsman.

Paul lived this way for 20 years. Just after his 21st birthday, the Winter of the Blue Snow settled in. Temperatures dropped to more than 60 degrees below zero. Even the snow turned blue from the cold. But Paul thought it was beautiful.

By the next morning, the ox was fine. But his coat remained bright blue forever. Paul called his new friend Babe. From that day on, Paul and Babe were never apart. They still share adventures together, even today.

Initial Blends: sp, st, sw, scr, spl, spr, str

Circle the consonant blend that will complete **both** words correctly.
Write the blend on the lines.

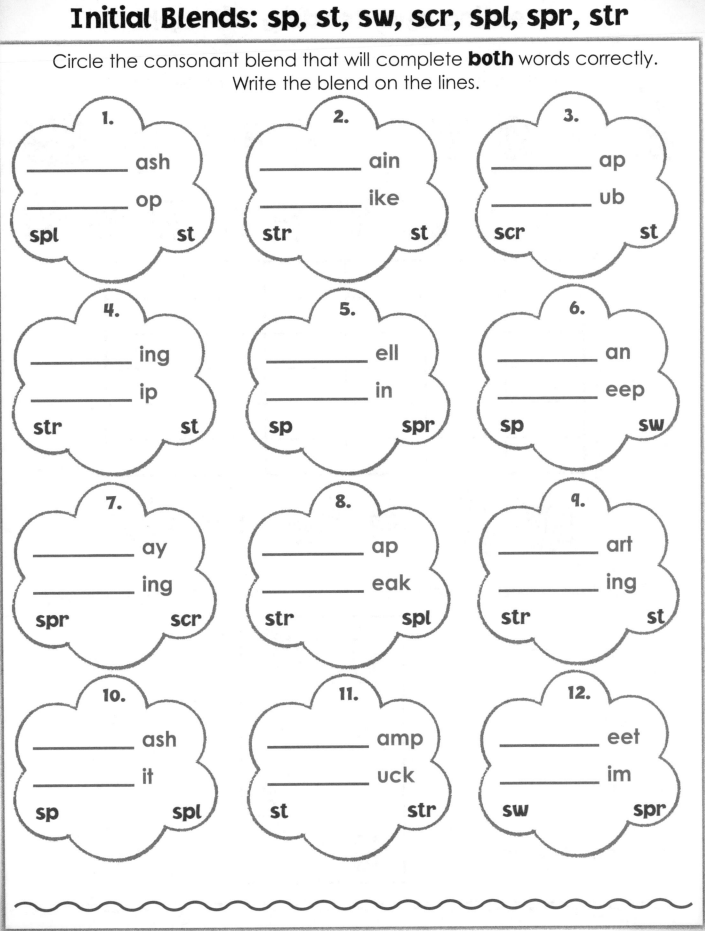

1.
_____ ash
_____ op
spl   st

2.
_____ ain
_____ ike
str   st

3.
_____ ap
_____ ub
scr   st

4.
_____ ing
_____ ip
str   st

5.
_____ ell
_____ in
sp   spr

6.
_____ an
_____ eep
sp   sw

7.
_____ ay
_____ ing
spr   scr

8.
_____ ap
_____ eak
str   spl

9.
_____ art
_____ ing
str   st

10.
_____ ash
_____ it
sp   spl

11.
_____ amp
_____ uck
st   str

12.
_____ eet
_____ im
sw   spr

Creating and Reading a Graph

Make a graph to tell about Farmer Mac's farm.
Color one square for each animal in the picture.

Complete the statements by circling the correct picture in each box.

A. Farmer Mac has more   than   .

B. Farmer Mac has fewer   than   .

C. Farmer Mac has fewer   than   .

D. Farmer Mac has more   than   .

Vowel Sounds

Sometimes two vowels together make one sound. One letter is silent.
Cut and paste each picture below the correct long vowel sound.

ā	ē	ō	ū

snail	loaf	hay	sheep
seal	train	goat	clue
fruit	blue	boat	peach

Vowel Sound ai/ay

When a word has two vowels together, the first vowel is usually long and the second vowel is silent. The **long a** sound can be spelled **ai** or **ay**.

Print the missing letters **ai** or **ay**. Read the words.

s _____   t _____ l   w _____   t s t _____

Complete the sentences using the words above.

1. I sure hope we can _____ overnight.

2. What animal has the longest _____ ?

Vowel Sound oa

The letters **oa** make the **long o** sound.

Read each word. Make a new word by adding the letter **a** after the letter **o**. Write the new word on the line. Read the new word aloud.

1. cot _____   2. bot _____   3. got _____

Read each set of words. Circle the word that has the **long o** sound.

4. tot   toad   tide   5. bite   bat   boat

6. moat   meat   mate   7. sock   soak   seek

Mixed Math Problems

Solve the problems. Circle the largest answer. Underline the smallest.

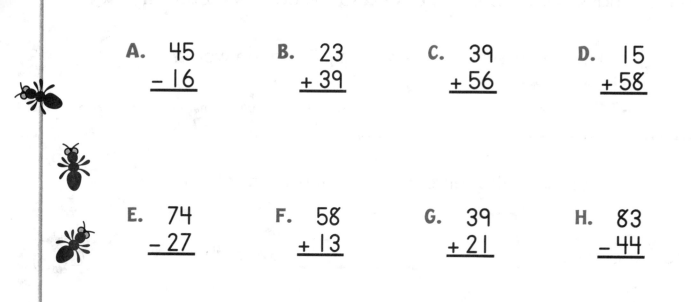

A. $\begin{array}{r} 45 \\ -16 \\ \hline \end{array}$ B. $\begin{array}{r} 23 \\ +39 \\ \hline \end{array}$ C. $\begin{array}{r} 39 \\ +56 \\ \hline \end{array}$ D. $\begin{array}{r} 15 \\ +58 \\ \hline \end{array}$

E. $\begin{array}{r} 74 \\ -27 \\ \hline \end{array}$ F. $\begin{array}{r} 58 \\ +13 \\ \hline \end{array}$ G. $\begin{array}{r} 39 \\ +21 \\ \hline \end{array}$ H. $\begin{array}{r} 83 \\ -44 \\ \hline \end{array}$

Phonics

Vowel Sound ea/ee

When a word has two vowels together, the first vowel is usually long and the second is silent. The **long e** sound can be spelled as **ea** or **ee**.

Print **ea** or **ee** to complete each word.

b _ _ t   b _ _   wh _ l   sh _ p

dr _ m   f _ _ t   tr _ _   l _ _ f

Place Value (Hundreds)

Numbers with three digits can be grouped
into sets of **hundreds**, **tens**, and **ones**.

254   is the same as   **2 hundreds**, **5 tens**, and **4 ones.**

Write each group of hundreds, tens, and ones as a number.

A.   **4** hundreds,   **6** tens,   and **3** ones   is   **463** .

B.   **5** hundreds,   **9** tens,   and **6** ones   is   _____ .

C.   **3** hundreds,   **2** tens,   and **7** ones   is   _____ .

D.   **2** hundreds,   **3** tens,   and **4** ones   is   _____ .

Vowel Sound ue/ui

The letters **ue** and **ui** make the **long u** sound.

Say the name of each picture. Circle the word that is spelled correctly.

1.   glui
     glue

2.   fruit
     fruet

3.   suat
     suit

Choose a word from the word list to complete each sentence.

Word List
glue
fruit
fuel
Sue

4. My best friend's name is _____ .

5. Cars need _____ to make them go.

Vowel Digraph oo

The letters **oo** can make the sound you hear in **food**
or the sound you hear in **look**.

Say the words in the word list. Listen to the **oo** sounds
they make. Write the words in the correct row.

Word List

school

foot

hook

tooth

1. food - - - - - - - - - -   - - - - - - - - - -

2. look - - - - - - - - - -   - - - - - - - - - -

Read the words. Circle the word in each row
that has the same vowel sound as the first word.

3. zoo   poor   pool   4. good   loot   took

5. crook   foot   scoop   6. room   goose   cook

Place Value (Hundreds)

Read each number. Circle the number in the hundreds place. Underline the number in the tens place. Draw a box around the number in the ones place.

A. 653   B. 594   C. 215   D. 726

E. 220   F. 125   G. 196   H. 967

Group each number into hundreds, tens, and ones.

I. 653 is _____ hundreds, _____ tens, and _____ ones.

J. 999 is _____ hundreds, _____ tens, and _____ ones.

K. 422 is _____ hundreds, _____ tens, and _____ ones.

L. 387 is _____ hundreds, _____ tens, and _____ ones.

Vowel Sound Review

Circle the vowel pair that completes each word correctly.

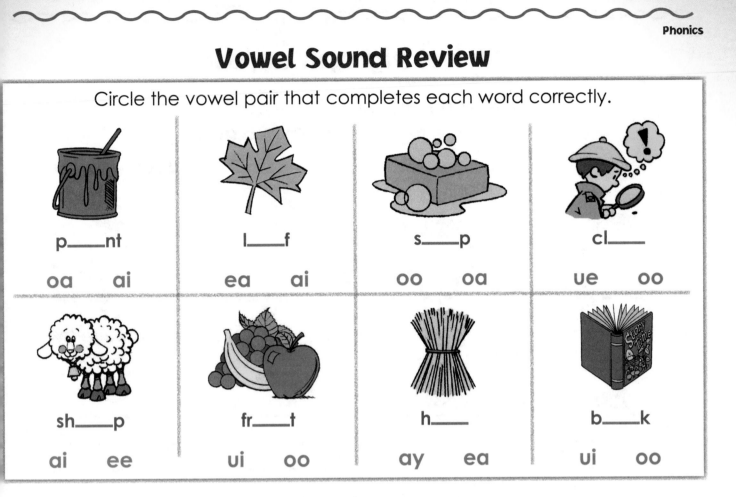

p___nt — oa   ai

l___f — ea   ai

s___p — oo   oa

cl___ — ue   oo

sh___p — ai   ee

fr___t — ui   oo

h___ — ay   ea

b___k — ui   oo

Vowel Diphthong oi/oy

The vowels **oi** and **oy** spell the same sound.
Compare the words **boil** and **boy**.

Complete each word by writing **oi** or **oy** on the lines.

1. n_____se

2. t_____

3. l_____al

4. b_____l

Circle the word that names each picture.

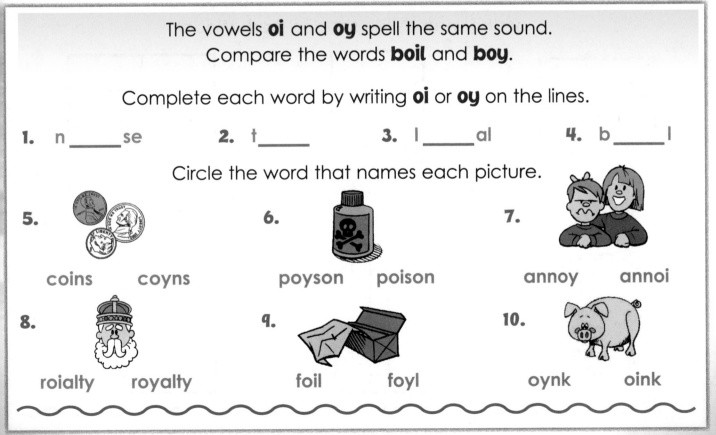

5. coins   coyns

6. poyson   poison

7. annoy   annoi

8. roialty   royalty

9. foil   foyl

10. oynk   oink

Vowel Digraph au/aw

The vowels **au** and **aw** spell the same sound.
Compare the words **fawn** and **auto**.

Say the picture name. If the vowel sound is the same as in **auto**, write **au**. If not, leave the space blank.

_____ to   _____ tumn   cl _____ n   c _____ ght

Say the picture name. If the vowel sound is the same as in **fawn**, write **aw**. If not, leave the space blank.

f _____ n   str _____   s _____   cl _____ d

Identifying Fractions

Circle the fraction that names the shaded part of each whole shape.

A. $\frac{1}{2}$ $\frac{1}{4}$ $\frac{1}{10}$

B. $\frac{1}{2}$ $\frac{1}{4}$ $\frac{1}{3}$

C. $\frac{1}{10}$ $\frac{1}{3}$ $\frac{1}{8}$

Write the fraction that shows the shaded part of each whole shape.

D. _____   E. _____   F. _____

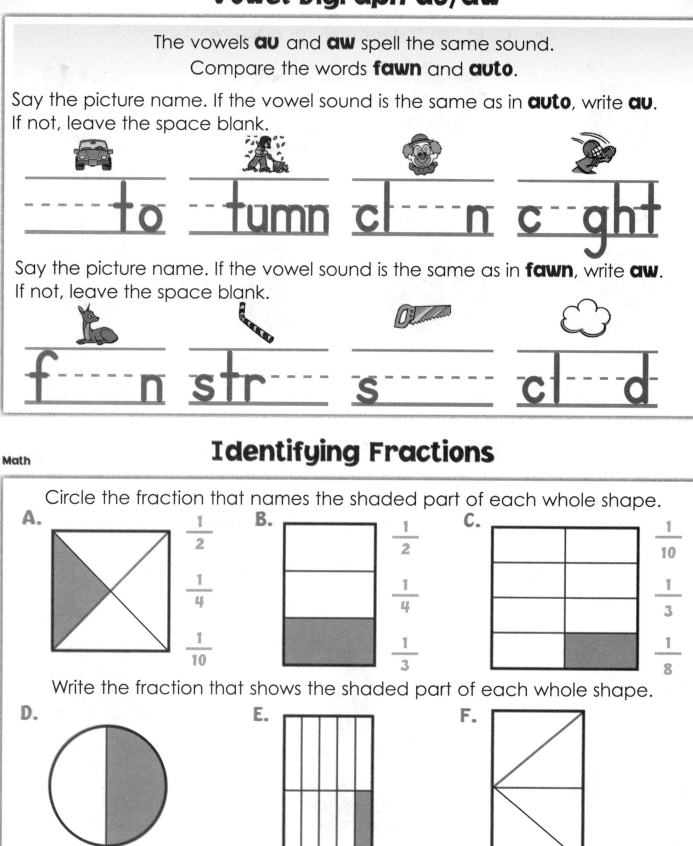

Matching Fractions

Draw a line to match each shape on the left to the
shape on the right that shows the same fraction.

Vowel Sound ow

The letters **ow** can make two different sounds.
Compare the words **cow** and **snow**.
Circle the pictures whose names contain the same
vowel sound as the first word in each group.

cow

snow

Compound Words

Choose a word from the word list to fit each description.

Word List

oatmeal	bookworm	rainbow	beehive

1. a display of colors after the rain: _____

2. a breakfast food: _____

3. a person who loves to read: _____

4. a home for bees: _____

Three-Digit Addends (with Regrouping)

Add the ones first.
5 + 3 = 8

hundreds	tens	ones
1	9	5
+ 6	4	3
		8

Then, add the tens.
9 + 4 = 13

hundreds	tens	ones
1	9	5
+ 6	4	3
	13	8

Write the 3 in the tens place. Regroup the 1 into the hundreds place.

hundreds	tens	ones
¹ 1	9	5
+ 6	4	3
	3	8

Add the hundreds.
1 + 1 + 6 = 8
The sum is 838.

hundreds	tens	ones
¹ 1	9	5
+ 6	4	3
8	3	8

Find the sum. Remember to regroup.

A. 645
   + 173

B. 218
   + 691

C. 724
   + 184

D. 296
   + 652

E. 552
   + 283

F. 460
   + 288

G. 121
   + 695

H. 776
   + 152

I. 157
   + 662

J. 336
   + 491

Color by Vowel Sound

Color the picture according to the sound of each word.

oi/oy = red

ow (cow) = blue

au/aw = yellow

ow (snow) = green

Three-Digit Story Problems

Write the addition problem in the box to solve each story problem.
Circle the clue words that tell you to add.

A.
Wanda completed 175 math problems in one week. Andy completed 217 problems. How many problems did they finish altogether?

B.
There are 358 sheep in a field. There are 519 sheep in another field. What is the sum of sheep in both fields?

Adverbs

Adverbs are words that tell **how**, **when**, or **where**.
Many adverbs that describe verbs end in **ly.**

She played outside.
The crowd cheered loudly.
Circle the adverb in each sentence.

1. Tony ran fast to catch the dog.

2. We can play tomorrow.

3. The girl sang softly.

4. Ling held the baby carefully.

5. We had a big test yesterday.

6. The boys sang very loudly.

7. The little boy acted politely.

8. The tiny worm crawled slowly.

9. The balloon floated upward.

10. We will have to call Sam later.

Reading Directions

1. Draw two birds in the tree farthest to the left.
2. Put a squirrel in the tree farthest to the right.
3. Draw a baby bear next to the big bear.
4. Color the two fish in the stream yellow.
5. Circle each animal that has fur.
6. Draw a box around each animal that does not have fur.
7. Color the tree that does not have animals in it.
8. Color the animals near the stream.

Synonyms and Antonyms

Synonyms are words that have the same or similar meanings.
Antonyms are words that have opposite meanings.

In each row, underline the synonym and circle the antonym.

1.	big	large	little	dog
2.	fast	slow	car	quick
3.	glad	silly	sad	happy
4.	smile	grin	mouth	frown

Vertical Number Sentences

Write each number sentence vertically in the box. Find the sum.

A. 566 + 183 = ____

B. 162 + 245 = ____

C. 363 + 574 = ____

Make up your own problems. Find the sums.

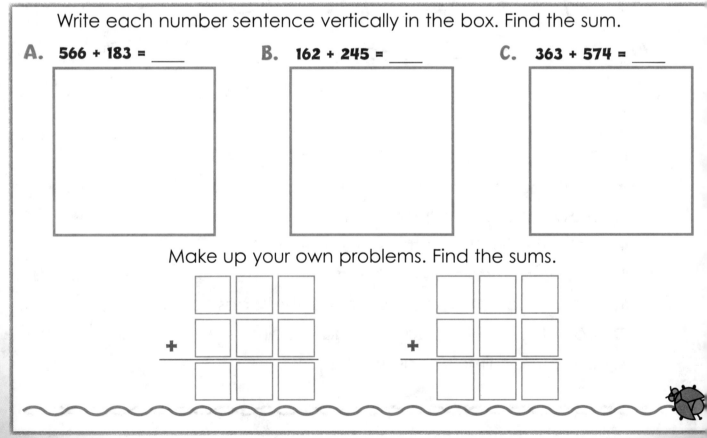

Subtraction Review

Find the difference. Circle each problem that uses regrouping.
Time yourself. How quickly can you solve the problems?

A. 82
   − 27

B. 54
   − 21

C. 23
   − 9

D. 46¢
   − 18¢

E. 57
   − 29

F. 27¢
   − 15¢

G. 48
   − 19

H. 37
   − 27

Telling Sentences

A **telling sentence** tells a complete thought.
A telling sentence begins with a capital letter and ends with a period.

Frank plays the piano.   **My name is Alice Rose.**

Read each sentence below. If it is a telling sentence, write a **T** on the line.
If it is not, leave the line blank.

_____ **1.** We went to the playground.   _____ **2.** What is your sister's name?

_____ **3.** Will you please help Lana?   _____ **4.** Spot is a good dog.

Rewrite the telling sentence below using a capital letter and period.

5. we went to the new mall

Missing Numbers (Hundreds)

Write the missing numbers in each row.

A. 748 _____ _____ _____ _____ 753

B. 397 _____ 399 _____ _____ _____

C. 600 _____ _____ _____ 604 _____

D. 991 _____ _____ _____ _____ 996

Count by 5s. Begin at 140. Stop at 240.

Writing Compound Sentences

Write a compound sentence about the things listed below.

1. a snowman and a snow fort

_____

- -

_____

2. a gift and a party

_____

- -

_____

3. your teacher and best friend

_____

- -

_____

Subtraction Review

Find the difference. Remember to regroup.

A. $\begin{array}{r} 38 \\ -19 \\ \hline \end{array}$
B. $\begin{array}{r} 42 \\ -17 \\ \hline \end{array}$
C. $\begin{array}{r} 95 \\ -39 \\ \hline \end{array}$
D. $\begin{array}{r} 52 \\ -13 \\ \hline \end{array}$

E. $\begin{array}{r} 27 \\ -18 \\ \hline \end{array}$
F. $\begin{array}{r} 67 \\ -39 \\ \hline \end{array}$
G. $\begin{array}{r} 55 \\ -18 \\ \hline \end{array}$
H. $\begin{array}{r} 48 \\ -29 \\ \hline \end{array}$

BONUS

Find the largest difference and the smallest difference on the page. Subtract the smallest difference from the largest difference.

Asking Sentences

An **asking sentence** asks a question.
It begins with a capital letter and ends with a question mark.

Would you like to come out and play?   **How are you?**

Read each pair of sentences. Circle the asking sentence.

1. I have a new coat.

Did you get a new coat?

2. Who is your teacher?

My teacher is Mrs. Jones.

Rewrite the sentence below as an asking sentence.

3. The cat can run quickly.

_____

- -

_____

Exclamatory Sentences

An **exclamatory sentence** tells something with strong feeling or excitement. Exclamatory sentences begin with a capital letter and end with an exclamation point.

I am excited!   **Ouch!**

Read each sentence. If it is an exclamatory sentence, write **!** on the line. If it is not, leave the line blank.

_____ **1.** What a surprise!   _____ **2.** Wow!   _____ **3.** My name is Amy.

Write an exclamatory sentence about the word below.

4. lightning

_____

- -

_____

Addition Review

Add. Regroup as needed.
Color the dinosaur egg blue if the sum is less than 250.
Color the egg green if the sum is greater than 250.

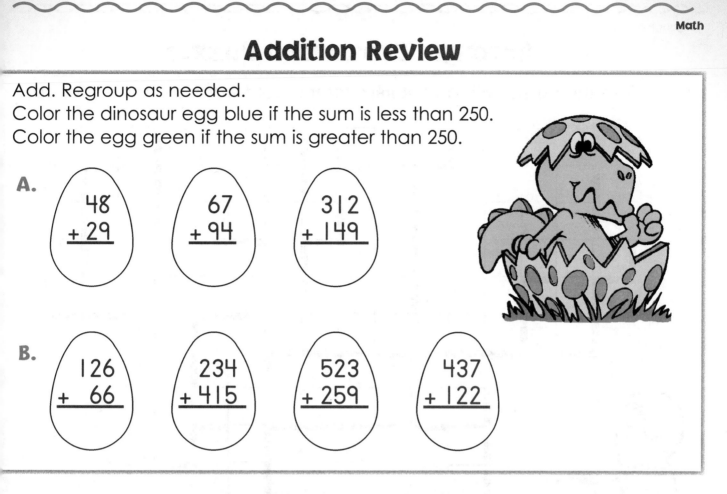

A.

$$48 + 29$$

$$67 + 94$$

$$312 + 149$$

B.

$$126 + 66$$

$$234 + 415$$

$$523 + 259$$

$$437 + 122$$

Ending Punctuation

Read each sentence. Write the correct ending punctuation on the line.

1. I like to skate in the winter ____

2. Some people ice-skate indoors ____

3. The pond freezes when it snows ____

4. Would you like to go ice-skating ____

5. Wow, that would be fun ____

6. Don't forget to wear a warm coat ____

7. Boy, it is cold outside ____

Antonym Crossword Puzzle

Complete the puzzle with an **antonym** for the bold word in each sentence.

Across

1. The meat in the dish is **cooked**.
8. Do you think that raccoon is **tame**?
9. Tamika is always **early** to school.
10. My grandmother is very **sick**.
12. Everyone who is going on the trip is **absent**.
14. A vacant house is a very **safe** place to be.
15. This has been the **best** day of my life.

Down

2. My brother **never** finishes the food on his plate.
3. The bulb in that lamp is very **dim**.
4. The children were very **noisy** today.
5. Charlene wore a very **fancy** dress today.
6. There are so **few** fish in the aquarium.
7. The water is very **shallow** at this end of the pool.
11. These pants feel too **tight**.
13. Will you **lead** me through the fun house?
14. The grass is very **wet** this morning.

Articles

The words **a**, **an**, and **the** are called **articles**.
Articles are sometimes used in front of nouns in sentences.

- **A** is used before a singular noun that begins with a consonant.

  A bat flew in the sky.

- **An** is used before a singular noun that begins with a vowel.

  An apple fell from the tree.

- **The** is used when you are talking about a specific item.
  The may be used in front of singular or plural nouns.

  The oranges are in the bag.

Use **a** ar **an** to complete each sentence.

1. _____ kite flew in the sky.

2. _____ elephant ate a peanut.

3. I went to _____ dance.

4. I need _____ orange crayon.

Circle the correct article in each sentence.

5. Larry plays (the   a) drums.

6. I want (an   a) tape.

7. (An   A) bird is flying overhead.

8. Do you see (the   an) bus stop?

Write a sentence that uses the articles **a** and **the**.

_____

_____

Write a sentence using the article **an**.

_____

_____

Proofreading Practice

Find and circle the **10** mistakes in the story.
Write the story again and correct the mistakes.

Last sumer i went to vst Tim at the lake. we went fshing. We
went so far out in the lak that the tres and howses lookt very little.
I caught ate fish.

The Case
of the
Missing Lunch

It was a crisp, spring morning. Alicia's father pulled up to the school and stopped.

"Have a good day, Kiddo."

"Thanks, Dad. See you later!"

Alicia stepped out of the car and closed the door. She waved as her father pulled away.

1

Alicia and Kelly raced each other to the playground. They set down their backpacks and lunches, then hopped on the monkey bars.

The girls swung, flipped, and hung upside down until their faces turned red. Then, they heard the bell ring.

3

"Hey, Alicia!" a voice called from behind.
Alicia turned to see her best friend Kelly
walking towards her.
"Hi!" Alicia smiled. "It's still early. Do you want
to hang out on the playground until the bell
rings?"
"Sure," said Kelly. "Let's go!"

2

As the girls stopped to pick up their bags,
Alicia said, "Hey! Who stole my lunch?"
"What do you mean?" asked Kelly.
"Well, I had a lunch 15 minutes ago. Now it's
gone!"
"I didn't see anyone else out here. That's
really weird."
"Yeah, I know. But we'd better get to class.
Mr. Clark hates it when people are late."

4

The girls ran inside and sat down. From her desk, Alicia looked around the room. The other kids were still talking and laughing.

"One of them must have stolen my lunch," Alicia said to herself. But who? She thought for a minute. "I know. It must have been Max—he's always bullying me around."

5

"Oh, really?" Alicia sneered. "Then, how do you explain this?" She reached into his desk and pulled out a lunch bag. It looked just like hers. But when she opened it, Alicia found only chips, candy, and a can of soda. It was not her lunch. "Oops!" she said, biting her lip. "Sorry."

7

Alicia stood up and walked over to Max's desk. He grunted at her, then turned back to his friends.

"Hey, Max," Alicia said, "give me back my lunch. I know you took it."

"Huh?" said Max. "Why would I steal your lunch? I wouldn't touch that healthy junk with a 10-foot pole."

6

Just then, Alicia heard a loud noise outside. She turned to look out the window and saw a big, black crow. It was carrying a lunch bag. On the bag she could see a big letter A.

The mystery was solved. Alicia had found her missing lunch.

8

End Mark Review

A **telling sentence** ends with a period.
An **asking sentence** ends with a question mark.
An **exclamatory sentence** ends with an exclamation point.

Fill in the missing punctuation marks. Then, circle the correct letter: **T** for a telling sentence, **A** for an asking sentence, or **E** for an exclamatory sentence.

1. Why is the sky blue____

   T   A   E

2. Hooray, school is out____

   T   A   E

3. Sue and Betty are friends____

   T   A   E

4. How much does this book cost____

   T   A   E

5. Is there any more pizza left____

   T   A   E

6. Look out____

   T   A   E

Mixed-Up Math

Math

Solve. Regroup if needed.

$$386 + 255$$

$$397 + 324$$

$$64 - 48$$

$$596 + 236$$

$$83 - 58$$

$$369 + 148$$

Find and circle the two-digit numbers less than 50.
Look across and down.

2	2	7	4	5
5	6	3	8	1
4	3	0	1	3
3	6	8	5	6
7	3	9	1	3

How many did you find?

Punctuation Review

Read the letter below. End each sentence with a period,
a question mark, or an exclamation point as needed.

Dear Marni,

   Hello   How is your family   I miss you very much   My mom
and dad said we will visit you soon I am excited   What will we do
for fun   I like to swim and fish

See you soon

Your friend,

Keisha

Story Problems

Solve each problem. Cross out the fact you do not need.

A.
Donna checked out 12 books about dogs. Mark checked out 9 books about birds. Luke checked out 10 books about flowers.

How many animal books did they check out in all?

B.
Debbie read 23 mystery books. She gave her brother 19 new books. She read 18 romance books.

How many books did Debbie read altogether?

C.
Helena got 17 books about cats. Brian got 24 books about the law. Helena loves her 4 cats!

How many more books did Brian get than Helena?

Math Chains

Add or subtract from left to right.

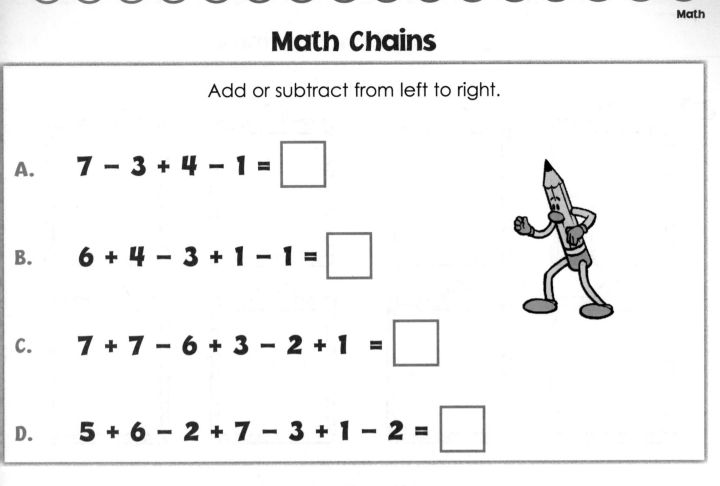

A. 7 − 3 + 4 − 1 = ☐

B. 6 + 4 − 3 + 1 − 1 = ☐

C. 7 + 7 − 6 + 3 − 2 + 1 = ☐

D. 5 + 6 − 2 + 7 − 3 + 1 − 2 = ☐

Contraction Match

Draw a line to match each pair of words with the correct contraction.

1. he had	aren't
2. I am	I'll
3. are not	she's
4. it has	they're
5. she is	he'd
6. I will	couldn't
7. they are	you've
8. you have	I'm
9. I would	it's
10. could not	I'd

Writing Contractions

Write the correct **contraction** for each pair of words.

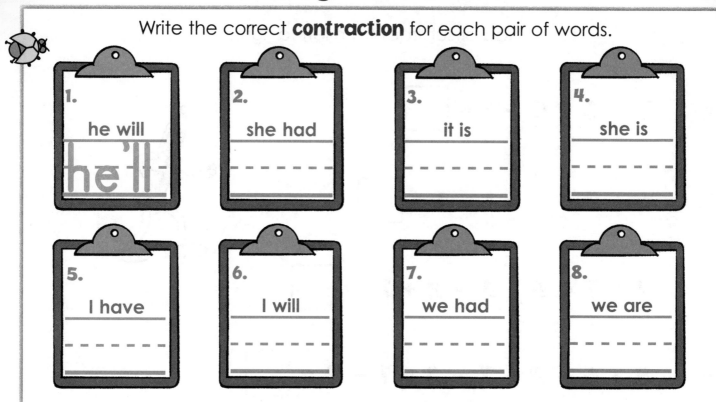

1. he will — he'll
2. she had
3. it is
4. she is

5. I have
6. I will
7. we had
8. we are

Adding Money Using Decimal Points

Line up the decimal points to add money.

A. $1.73
   + $3.37

B. $6.15
   + $2.34

C. $2.29
   + $0.56

D. $4.18
   + $2.25

E. $2.01
   + $0.89

F. $2.57
   + $4.26

G. $4.61
   + $3.75

H. $6.76
   + $2.27

BONUS

If you have $4.63 and a friend has $2.18, how much money would you have altogether? _____

Words into Math

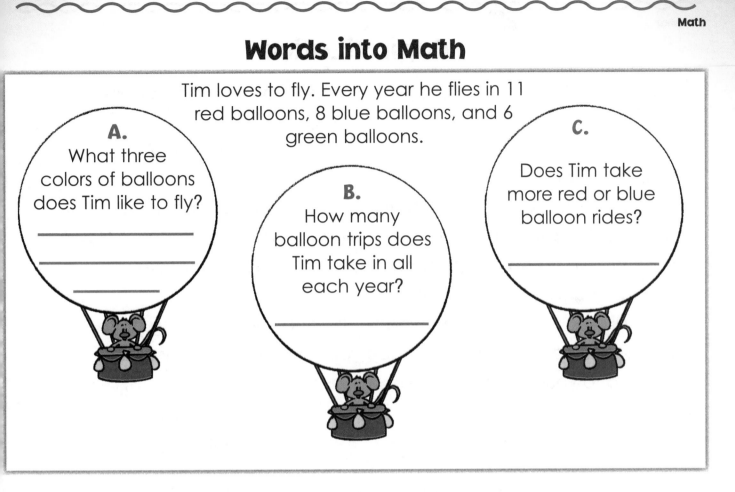

Tim loves to fly. Every year he flies in 11 red balloons, 8 blue balloons, and 6 green balloons.

A. What three colors of balloons does Tim like to fly?

_____

_____

_____

B. How many balloon trips does Tim take in all each year?

_____

C. Does Tim take more red or blue balloon rides?

_____

One-Two-Three Syllables

Sort the words in the word list. Print each one-syllable word under the bear. Print each two-syllable word under the lion. Print each three-syllable word under the elephant.

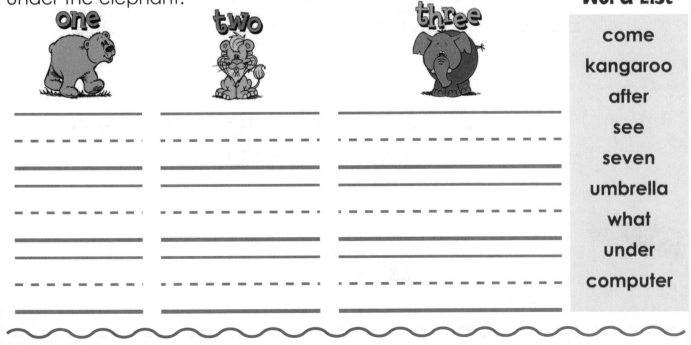

Word List

come

kangaroo

after

see

seven

umbrella

what

under

computer

Capitalization

Read the letter below. Circle each word that should be capitalized.

june 5, 2002

dear aunt amy,

My last day of school was friday. Mom and i are going to orlando, florida. Then, in july, i am going to visit uncle rodney in New york. We will spend independence day on Coney island. are you taking a vacation this summer?

do you like to go swimming? abby and i go swimming at the franklin club every thursday. i hope you have a fun summer. I look forward to your visit in december.

yours truly,

albert

Math

Three-Digit Subtraction Review

Subtract to find each difference.

A.	824 − 525	B.	976 − 387	C.	442 − 184	D.	521 − 342

E.	755 − 297	F.	613 − 425	G.	847 − 369	H.	410 −132

BONUS

Write a problem to show **566** subtracted from **655**. Write the difference.

Map Skills

Look at the map. Follow the directions below.
Use the map key to help you find the places on the map.

1. Color the school red.
2. Color the park green.
3. Circle the lake.
4. Put an **X** on Apple Lane.
5. Draw a lake below the school.
6. Draw a park near the lake that you drew.

Map Key

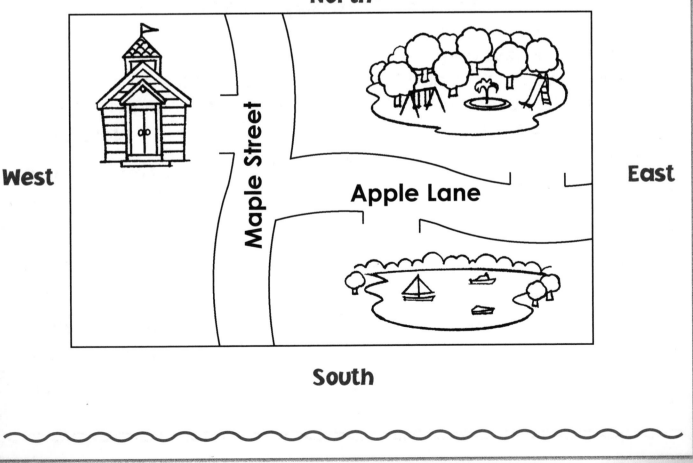

North

West

East

South

Prefixes: un- and re-

The prefix **un-** means **not.** The prefix **re-** means **again**. Add **un-** or **re-** to the beginning of these words to complete these sentences.

She is _____ able to find her backpack.

Dave had to _____ write his essay.

Scott _____ washed his fork after dropping it.

Zara was _____ happy it rained during her soccer game.

Suffixes: -less, -ness

The suffix **less** or **ness** can be added to each of the words from the word list. Decide which suffix to add to each word and print the new word on a line under the correct suffix. When a word ends in **y**, change the **y** to **i** before adding a suffix.

Word List

home	neat
sweet	harm
odor	good
lonely	hope
happy	care
soft	sleep
sad	help
color	sick

-less

1. _____
2. _____
3. _____
4. _____
5. _____
6. _____
7. _____
8. _____

-ness

1. _____
2. _____
3. _____
4. _____
5. _____
6. _____
7. _____
8. _____

Answer Key

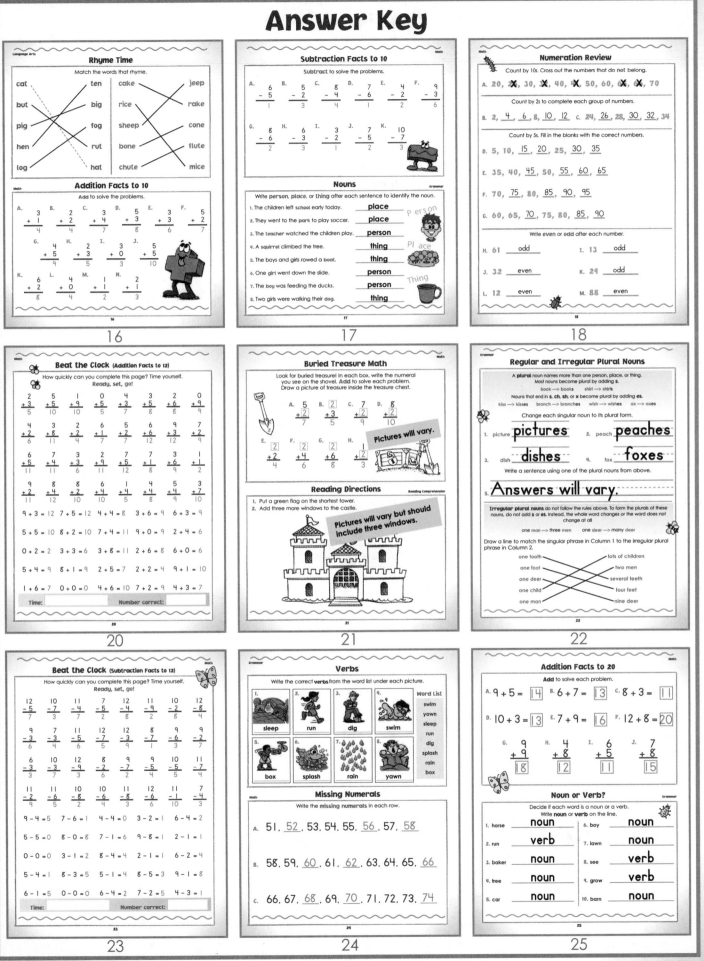

Rhyme Time
Language Arts

Match the words that rhyme.

cat — ten
but — big
pig — fog
hen — rut
log — hat

cake — jeep
rice — rake
sheep — cone
bone — flute
chute — mice

Addition Facts to 10
Math

Add to solve the problems.

A. 3 + 1 = 4 B. 2 + 2 = 4 C. 3 + 4 = 7 D. 5 + 3 = 8 E. 3 + 3 = 6 F. 5 + 2 = 7

G. 4 + 5 = 9 H. 2 + 3 = 5 I. 3 + 0 = 3 J. 5 + 5 = 10

K. 6 + 2 = 8 L. 4 + 0 = 4 M. 1 + 1 = 2 N. 2 + 1 = 3

16

Subtraction Facts to 10
Math

Subtract to solve the problems.

A. 6 − 5 = 1 B. 5 − 2 = 3 C. 8 − 4 = 4 D. 7 − 6 = 1 E. 4 − 2 = 2 F. 9 − 3 = 6

G. 8 − 6 = 2 H. 6 − 3 = 3 I. 3 − 2 = 1 J. 7 − 5 = 2 K. 10 − 7 = 3

Nouns
Grammar

Write person, place, or thing after each sentence to identify the noun.

1. The children left school early today. **place**
2. They went to the park to play soccer. **place**
3. The teacher watched the children play. **person**
4. A squirrel climbed the tree. **thing**
5. The boys and girls rowed a boat. **thing**
6. One girl went down the slide. **person**
7. The boy was feeding the ducks. **person**
8. Two girls were walking their dog. **thing**

Person
Place
Thing

17

Numeration Review
Math

Count by 10s. Cross out the numbers that do not belong.

A. 20, ~~25~~, 30, ~~36~~, 40, ~~41~~, 50, 60, ~~61~~, ~~65~~, 70

Count by 2s to complete each group of numbers.

B. 2, **4**, **6**, 8, **10**, 12 c. 24, **26**, 28, **30**, **32**, 34

Count by 5s. Fill in the blanks with the correct numbers.

D. 5, 10, **15**, **20**, 25, **30**, **35**

E. 35, 40, **45**, 50, **55**, **60**, 65

F. 70, **75**, 80, **85**, **90**, 95

G. 60, 65, **70**, 75, 80, **85**, **90**

Write even or odd after each number.

H. 61 **odd**   I. 13 **odd**

J. 32 **even**   K. 29 **odd**

L. 12 **even**   M. 88 **even**

18

Beat the Clock (Addition Facts to 12)
Math

How quickly can you complete this page? Time yourself.
Ready, set, go!

2 + 3 = 5 5 + 5 = 10 4 + 9 = 10 2 + 5 = 7 4 + 3 = 7 3 + 6 = 9 0 + 9 = 9

4 + 2 = 6 3 + 8 = 8 2 + 1 = 6 5 + 2 = 7 6 + 6 = 12 4 + 3 = 12 9 + 2 = 7

6 + 5 = 11 7 + 4 = 11 3 + 3 = 6 2 + 9 = 11 5 + 7 = 12 3 + 5 = 8 1 + 1 = 2

9 + 2 = 11 8 + 4 = 12 8 + 2 = 10 2 + 8 = 10 4 + 1 = 5 6 + 3 = 9 3 + 7 = 10

9 + 3 = 12 7 + 5 = 12 4 + 4 = 8 3 + 6 = 9 6 + 3 = 9

5 + 5 = 10 8 + 2 = 10 7 + 4 = 11 9 + 0 = 9 2 + 4 = 6

0 + 2 = 2 3 + 3 = 6 3 + 8 = 11 2 + 6 = 8 6 + 0 = 6

5 + 4 = 9 8 + 1 = 9 2 + 5 = 7 2 + 2 = 4 9 + 1 = 10

1 + 6 = 7 0 + 0 = 0 4 + 6 = 10 7 + 2 = 9 4 + 3 = 7

Time: _____   Number correct: _____

20

Buried Treasure Math
Math

Look for buried treasure in each box. Write the numeral you see on the shovel. Add to solve each problem.

A. 5 + 2 = 7 B. 2 + 2 = 4 C. 7 + 2 = 9 D. 8 + 2 = 10

E. 2 + 2 = 4 F. 2 + 2 = 4 G. 2 + 2 = 4 H. 1 + 2 = 3

Pictures will vary.

Reading Directions
Reading Comprehension

1. Put a green flag on the shortest tower.
2. Add three more windows to the castle.

Pictures will vary but should include three windows.

21

Regular and Irregular Plural Nouns
Grammar

A **plural** noun names more than one person, place, or thing. Most nouns become plural by adding **s**.

book --> books   shirt --> shirts

Nouns that end in **s, ch, sh,** or **x** become plural by adding **es.**

kiss --> kisses   branch --> branches   wish --> wishes   ax --> axes

Change each singular noun to its plural form.

1. picture **pictures**   2. peach **peaches**

3. dish **dishes**   4. fox **foxes**

Write a sentence using one of the plural nouns from above.

Answers will vary.

Irregular plural nouns do not follow the rules above. To form the plurals of these nouns, do not add **s** or **es**. Instead, the whole word changes or the word does not change at all.

one man --> three men   one deer --> many deer

Draw a line to match the singular phrase in Column 1 to the irregular plural phrase in Column 2.

one tooth — lots of children
one foot — two men
one deer — several teeth
one child — four feet
one man — nine deer

22

Beat the Clock (Subtraction Facts to 12)
Math

How quickly can you complete this page? Time yourself.
Ready, set, go!

12 − 5 = 7 10 − 7 = 3 11 − 4 = 7 7 − 5 = 2 11 − 2 = 9 10 − 2 = 8 12 − 8 = 4

9 − 3 = 6 7 − 3 = 4 11 − 5 = 6 12 − 7 = 5 12 − 3 = 9 8 − 6 = 2 9 − 2 = 7

6 − 3 = 3 10 − 9 = 1 12 − 5 = 7 8 − 2 = 6 9 − 7 = 2 9 − 5 = 4 10 − 7 = 7

11 − 2 = 9 11 − 6 = 5 10 − 6 = 4 10 − 6 = 4 11 − 8 = 3 12 − 6 = 6 11 − 4 = 7

9 − 4 = 5 7 − 6 = 1 4 − 4 = 0 3 − 2 = 1 6 − 4 = 2

5 − 5 = 0 8 − 0 = 8 7 − 1 = 6 9 − 8 = 1 2 − 1 = 1

0 − 0 = 0 3 − 1 = 2 8 − 4 = 4 2 − 1 = 1 6 − 2 = 4

5 − 4 = 1 7 − 3 = 4 5 − 4 = 1 8 − 5 = 3 9 − 1 = 8

6 − 1 = 5 0 − 0 = 0 6 − 4 = 2 7 − 2 = 5 4 − 3 = 1

Time: _____   Number correct: _____

23

Verbs
Grammar

Write the correct **verbs** from the word list under each picture.

1. sleep   2. run   3. dig   4. swim

5. box   6. splash   7. rain   8. yawn

Word List
swim
yawn
sleep
run
dig
splash
rain
box

Missing Numerals
Math

Write the missing numerals in each row.

A. 51, **52**, 53, 54, 55, **56**, 57, **58**

B. 58, 59, **60**, 61, **62**, 63, 64, 65, **66**

C. 66, 67, **68**, 69, **70**, 71, 72, 73, **74**

24

Addition Facts to 20
Math

Add to solve each problem.

A. 9 + 5 = 14   B. 6 + 7 = 13   C. 8 + 3 = 11

D. 10 + 3 = 13   E. 7 + 9 = 16   F. 12 + 8 = 20

G. 9 + 9 = 18   H. 4 + 8 = 12   I. 6 + 5 = 11   J. 7 + 8 = 15

Noun or Verb?
Grammar

Decide if each word is a noun or a verb. Write **noun** or **verb** on the line.

1. horse **noun**   6. boy **noun**
2. run **verb**   7. lawn **noun**
3. baker **noun**   8. see **verb**
4. tree **noun**   9. grow **verb**
5. car **noun**   10. barn **noun**

25

Answer Key

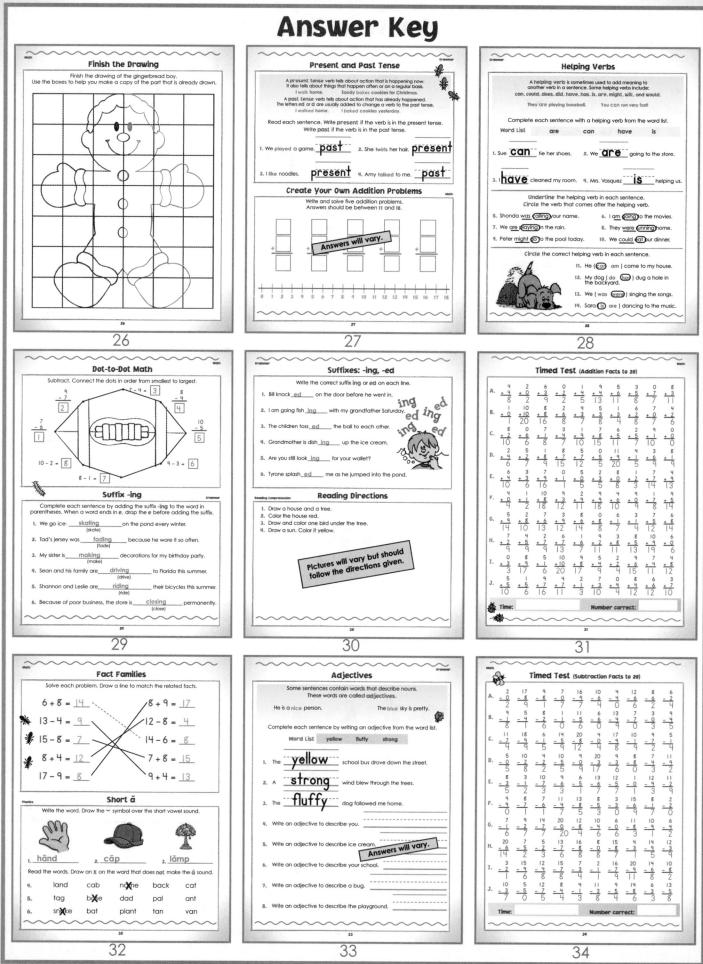

Answer Key

Number Words to 100

Numbers can be written as numerals or as words.

4	18	52	99
four	eighteen	fifty-two	ninety-nine

Draw a line to match each number word to the correct numeral.

A.
twenty-three — 99
seventy-five — 11
sixty-two — 23
ninety-nine — 32
eighteen — 18
thirty-two — 62
eleven — 75

B.
fifteen — 100
eighty-four — 84
forty-seven — 72
twenty-six — 15
fifty-three — 47
twelve — 53
one hundred — 26

Missy and Kim: A Story

Read the story. Match the question with the correct answer.

One cold, winter day Missy and Kim went for a walk in the woods. They saw a deer eating the bark of a tree. When Kim stepped on a twig, the deer suddenly ran away. The girls decided it was too cold to keep walking. They went home.

1. Who went for a walk? — the woods
2. What season was it? — Missy and Kim
3. What did the deer eat? — It was too cold.
4. Where did the girls go for a walk? — winter
5. Why did the girls go home? — bark of a tree

39

Short ĕ

Circle the word that names the picture.

desk / den / dark — (desk)
bang / bet / (bell)
(tent) / tan / ten
nest / (net) / nut

Write four words that have the short ĕ vowel sound.

Answers will vary.

Tic-Tac-Toe Math

Solve the problems. Find three answers in a row that match.

+
12 +5 = 17	8 +8 = 16	10 +5 = 15
6 +6 = 12	3 +7 = 10	8 +2 = 10
9 +6 = 15	9 +5 = 14	6 +6 = 12

−
11 −7 = 4	8 −6 = 6	10 −9 = 1
9 −4 = 5	10 −5 = 5	11 −6 = 5
18 −9 = 9	11 −9 = 2	10 −7 = 3

40

Addition Chart

Find the sums to complete the chart.

+	0	1	2	3	4	5	6	7	8	9
0	0	1	2	3	4	5	6	7	8	9
1	1	2	3	4	5	6	7	8	9	10
2	2	3	4	5	6	7	8	9	10	11
3	3	4	5	6	7	8	9	10	11	12
4	4	5	6	7	8	9	10	11	12	13
5	5	6	7	8	9	10	11	12	13	14
6	6	7	8	9	10	11	12	13	14	15
7	7	8	9	10	11	12	13	14	15	16
8	8	9	10	11	12	13	14	15	16	17
9	9	10	11	12	13	14	15	16	17	18

BRAIN BUILDER

Think of three numbers whose sum equals the center number in each triangle. Do not use 0.

5 8 13 12 4 3 | 6 8 15 3 14 7

41

Number Words

Circle the correct numeral for each number word.

A. forty-five — 54 (45)
B. eighty-one — 18 (81)
C. three — 30 (3)
D. fifty-eight — (58) 85
E. thirty — (30) 31
F. fifteen — (15) 50

BONUS Write the number words for the following numerals: 0, 20, 30, 40, 60, and 80.

| zero | twenty | thirty |
| forty | sixty | eighty |

Main Idea

Circle the main idea of each picture.

1.
(The mother feeds her babies.)
The birds have feathers.

2.
The raccoon's tail is long.
(The raccoon washes its food.)

3.
(The horse is fast.)
The horse won the race.

42

Alphabetical Order

Read the words in each jar. Write the words in alphabetical order on the lines below the jar.

nut / arm / foot / coat / basket

match / whale / cape / yard / shark

1. arm
2. basket
3. coat
4. foot
5. nut

1. cape
2. match
3. shark
4. whale
5. yard

43

Adding Three Single-Digit Addends

Add to solve each problem.

A. 1 + 4 + 5 = 10
B. 5 + 3 + 4 = 12
C. 1 + 9 + 6 = 16
D. 3 + 6 + 3 = 12
E. 9 + 3 + 5 = 17
F. 1 + 6 + 7 = 14
G. 5 + 4 + 6 = 15
H. 2 + 7 + 5 = 14
I. 4 + 1 + 5 = 10
J. 6 + 2 + 7 = 15

Complete the Sentence

Choose the best adjective from the word list to complete each sentence.

Word List
funny
six
red
hard
oak
flying
furry

1. His kite got caught in that _oak_ tree.
2. I can't believe you ate _six_ hot dogs!
3. At the circus, we laughed at the _funny_ clowns.
4. Jackie got a _red_ bike for Christmas.
5. My pillow is very _hard_ and lumpy.
6. The rabbits all had soft and _furry_ ears.

44

Subject and Predicate

Draw a line to connect the subject and predicate phrases in each set to form sentences that make sense.

1. The strong winds — A. uprooted three trees.
2. Our class — B. decoded the message.
3. The spy — C. will visit the fire station.

1. My little brother — A. have fun in art class.
2. The bumblebee — B. fell off his skateboard.
3. We — C. stung my sister.

Short ĭ

Print an i in each word. Read the word. Draw a short ⌣ symbol over each i.

wĭg pĭn pĭg fĭsh

Fill in the correct word from the word list to complete each sentence.

Word List
six
ink
kiss

1. The pen ran out of _ink_.
2. The boy gave the girl a _kiss_.
3. I have _six_ marbles.

45

Tall Sums

Add to solve each problem.

A. 4 + 8 + 6 = 18
B. 5 + 2 + 3 = 10
C. 3 + 7 + 3 = 13
D. 5 + 1 + 7 = 13
E. 3 + 8 + 4 = 15
F. 6 + 5 + 5 = 16

Write Your Own Subject Phrase

Add a subject phrase to complete each sentence.

1. _____ rode on the Ferris wheel.
2. _____ gave me some money.
3. _____ went to the circus.
4. _____ lifted the heavy weights.
5. _____ did some great magic tricks.
6. _____ bought lots of popcorn.
7. _____ threw the ball.

Answers will vary.

46

Place Value (Tens)

Numbers with two digits can be grouped into sets of tens and ones.

15 is the same as 1 ten and 5 ones

Circle each group of ten. Count how many ones are left over. Write the correct numbers.

A. 17 is _1_ ten and _7_ ones
B. 24 is _2_ tens and _4_ ones

Group each number into tens and ones.

C. 45 is _4_ tens and _5_ ones
D. 7 is _0_ tens and _7_ ones
E. 29 is _2_ tens and _9_ ones
F. 23 is _2_ tens and _3_ ones
G. 4 is _0_ tens and _4_ ones
H. 99 is _9_ tens and _9_ ones

Read the number at the beginning of each row. Rewrite each number as tens and ones.

I.	tens	ones
6	0	6
45	4	5
32	3	2
8	0	8
75	7	5

J.	tens	ones
27	2	7
51	5	1
40	4	0
5	0	5
33	3	3

47

Answer Key

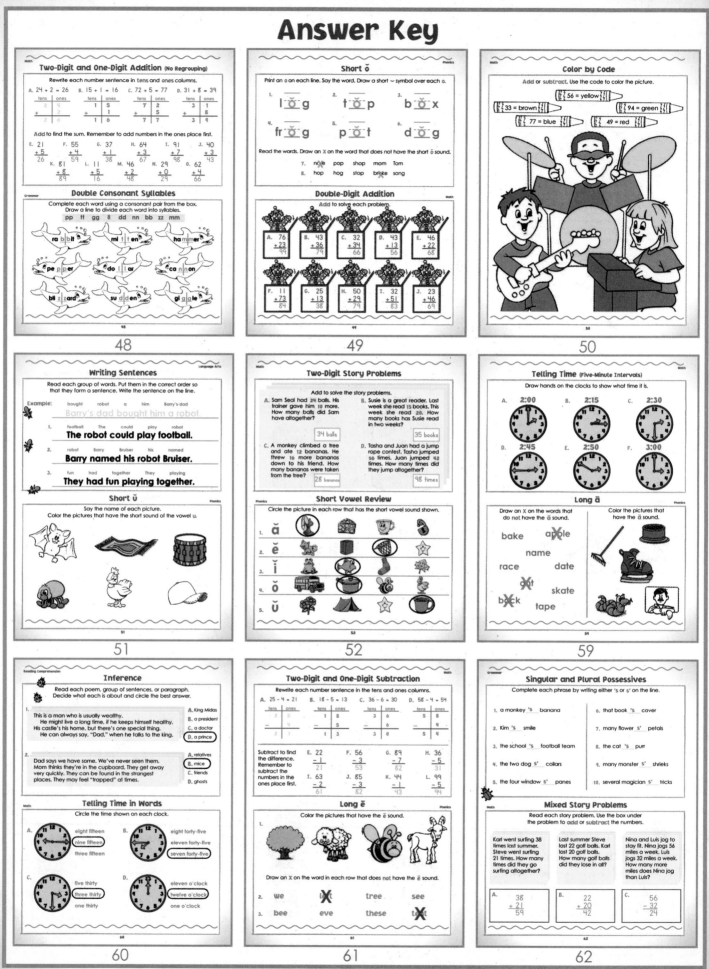

Two-Digit and One-Digit Addition (No Regrouping)

Rewrite each number sentence in tens and ones columns.

A. 24 + 2 = 26   B. 15 + 1 = 16   C. 72 + 5 = 77   D. 31 + 8 = 39

tens	ones
2	4
+	2
2	6

tens	ones
1	5
+	1
1	6

tens	ones
7	2
+	5
7	7

tens	ones
3	1
+	8
3	9

Add to find the sum. Remember to add numbers in the ones place first.

E. 21 +5 = 26   F. 55 +4 = 59   G. 37 +1 = 38   H. 64 +3 = 67   I. 91 +7 = 98   J. 40 +3 = 43

K. 81 +8 = 89   L. 11 +5 = 16   M. 46 +2 = 48   N. 29 +0 = 29   O. 62 +4 = 66

Double Consonant Syllables

Complete each word using a consonant pair from the box. Draw a line to divide each word into syllables.

pp tt gg ll dd nn bb zz mm

ra|bb|it   mi|tt|en   ha|mm|er

pe|pp|er   do|ll|ar   ca|nn|on

bli|zz|ard   su|dd|en   gi|gg|le

48

Short ŏ

Print an o on each line. Say the word. Draw a short ˘ symbol over each o.

1. lŏg   2. tŏp   3. bŏx

4. frŏg   5. pŏt   6. dŏg

Read the words. Draw an X on the word that does not have the short ŏ sound.

7. nose pop shop mom Tom

8. hop hog stop broke song

Double-Digit Addition

Add to solve each problem.

A. 76 +23 = 99   B. 43 +36 = 79   C. 32 +34 = 66   D. 43 +13 = 56   E. 46 +22 = 68

F. 11 +73 = 84   G. 25 +13 = 38   H. 50 +29 = 79   I. 32 +51 = 83   J. 23 +46 = 69

49

Color by Code

Add or subtract. Use the code to color the picture.

33 = brown   56 = yellow   94 = green   77 = blue   49 = red

50

Writing Sentences

Read each group of words. Put them in the correct order so that they form a sentence. Write the sentence on the line.

Example: bought robot a him Barry's dad
Barry's dad bought him a robot.

1. football The could play robot
The robot could play football.

2. robot Barry Bruiser his named
Barry named his robot Bruiser.

3. fun had together They playing
They had fun playing together.

Short ŭ

Say the name of each picture. Color the pictures that have the short sound of the vowel u.

51

Two-Digit Story Problems

Add to solve the story problems.

A. Sam Seal had 24 balls. His trainer gave him 10 more. How many balls did Sam have altogether?
34 balls

B. Susie is a great reader. Last week she read 15 books. This week she read 20. How many books has Susie read in two weeks?
35 books

C. A monkey climbed a tree and ate 12 bananas. He threw 16 more bananas down to his friend. How many bananas were taken from the tree?
28 bananas

D. Tasha and Juan had a jump rope contest. Tasha jumped 56 times. Juan jumped 42 times. How many times did they jump altogether?
98 times

Short Vowel Review

Circle the picture in each row that has the short vowel sound shown.

1. ă
2. ĕ
3. ĭ
4. ŏ
5. ŭ

52

Telling Time (Five-Minute Intervals)

Draw hands on the clocks to show what time it is.

A. 2:00   B. 2:15   C. 2:30

D. 2:45   E. 2:50   F. 3:00

Long ā

Draw an X on the words that do not have the ā sound.

bake   apXle

name

race   date

Xt   skate

bXck   tape

Color the pictures that have the ā sound.

59

Inference

Read each poem, group of sentences, or paragraph. Decide what each is about and circle the best answer.

1. This is a man who is usually wealthy. He might live a long time, if he keeps himself healthy. His castle's his home, but there's one special thing. He can always say, "Dad," when he talks to the king.
   A. King Midas
   B. a president
   C. a doctor
   D. a prince

2. Dad says we have some. We've never seen them. Mom thinks they're in the cupboard. They get away very quickly. They can be found in the strangest places. They may feel "trapped" at times.
   A. relatives
   B. mice
   C. friends
   D. ghosts

Telling Time in Words

Circle the time shown on each clock.

A. eight fifteen (nine fifteen) three fifteen

B. eight forty-five eleven forty-five (seven forty-five)

C. five thirty (three thirty) one thirty

D. eleven o'clock (twelve o'clock) one o'clock

60

Two-Digit and One-Digit Subtraction

Rewrite each number sentence in the tens and ones columns.

A. 25 - 4 = 21   B. 18 - 5 = 13   C. 36 - 6 = 30   D. 58 - 4 = 54

tens	ones
2	5
-	4
2	1

tens	ones
1	8
-	5
1	3

tens	ones
3	6
-	6
3	0

tens	ones
5	8
-	4
5	4

Subtract to find the difference. Remember to subtract the numbers in the ones place first.

E. 22 -1 = 21   F. 56 -3 = 53   G. 89 -7 = 82   H. 36 -5 = 31

I. 63 -2 = 61   J. 85 -3 = 82   K. 44 -1 = 43   L. 99 -5 = 94

Long ē

Color the pictures that have the ē sound.

1.

Draw an X on the word in each row that does not have the ē sound.

2. we iXt tree see

3. bee eve these teXt

61

Singular and Plural Possessives

Complete each phrase by writing either 's or s' on the line.

1. a monkey 's banana
2. Kim 's smile
3. the school 's football team
4. the two dog s' collars
5. the four window s' panes
6. that book 's cover
7. many flower s' petals
8. the cat 's purr
9. many monster s' shrieks
10. several magician s' tricks

Mixed Story Problems

Read each story problem. Use the box under the problem to add or subtract the numbers.

Karl went surfing 38 times last summer. Steve went surfing 21 times. How many times did they go surfing altogether?

Last summer Steve lost 22 golf balls. Karl lost 20 golf balls. How many golf balls did they lose in all?

Nina and Luis jog to stay fit. Nina jogs 56 miles a week. Luis jogs 32 miles a week. How many more miles does Nina jog than Luis?

A. 38 +21 = 59   B. 22 +20 = 42   C. 56 -32 = 24

62

Answer Key

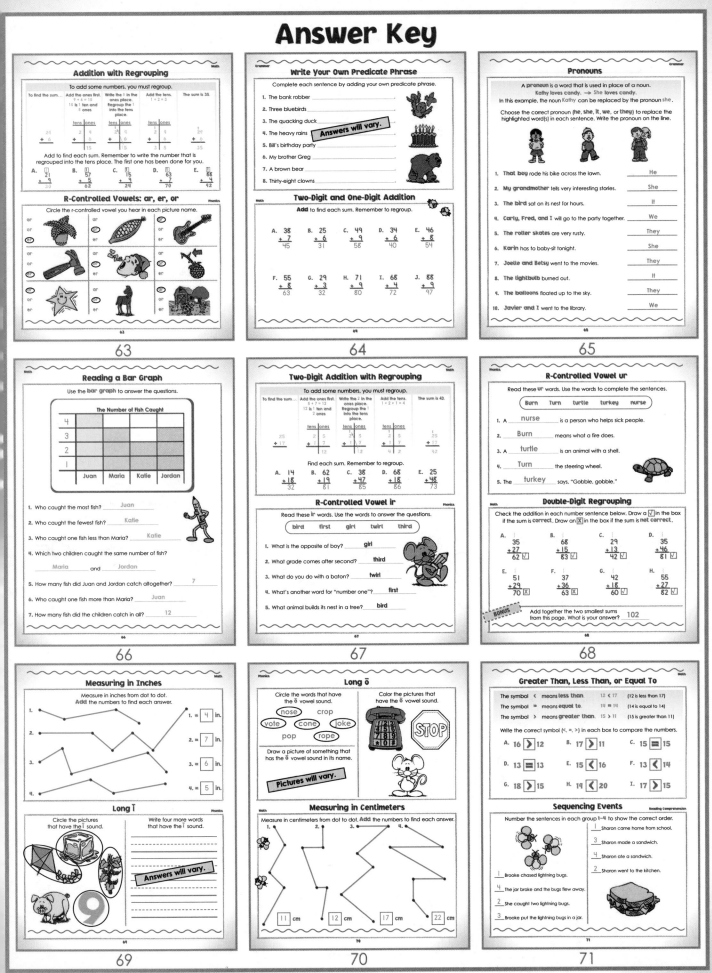

Addition with Regrouping

To add some numbers, you must regroup.

Add to find each sum. Remember to write the number that is regrouped into the tens place. The first one has been done for you.

A. 21 +5 = 26   B. +5   C. +9 = 24   D. 63 +7   E. 88 +4 = 42

R-Controlled Vowels: ar, er, or

Circle the r-controlled vowel you hear in each picture name.

63

Write Your Own Predicate Phrase

Complete each sentence by adding your own predicate phrase.

1. The bank robber
2. Three bluebirds
3. The quacking duck
4. The heavy rains
5. Bill's birthday party
6. My brother Greg
7. A brown bear
8. Thirty-eight clowns

Answers will vary.

Two-Digit and One-Digit Addition

Add to find each sum. Remember to regroup.

A. 38 +7 = 45   B. 25 +6 = 31   C. 49 +9 = 58   D. 34 +6 = 40   E. 46 +8 = 54

F. 55 +8 = 63   G. 29 +3 = 32   H. 71 +9 = 80   I. 68 +4 = 72   J. 88 +9 = 97

64

Pronouns

A pronoun is a word that is used in place of a noun.
Kathy loves candy. → She loves candy.
In this example, the noun Kathy can be replaced by the pronoun she.

Choose the correct pronoun (he, she, it, we, or they) to replace the highlighted word(s) in each sentence. Write the pronoun on the line.

1. That boy rode his bike across the lawn. — He
2. My grandmother tells very interesting stories. — She
3. The bird sat on its nest for hours. — It
4. Carly, Fred, and I will go to the party together. — We
5. The roller skates are very rusty. — They
6. Karin has to baby-sit tonight. — She
7. Joelle and Betsy went to the movies. — They
8. The lightbulb burned out. — It
9. The balloons floated up to the sky. — They
10. Javier and I went to the library. — We

65

Reading a Bar Graph

Use the bar graph to answer the questions.

The Number of Fish Caught
(Juan, Maria, Katie, Jordan)

1. Who caught the most fish? — Juan
2. Who caught the fewest fish? — Katie
3. Who caught one fish less than Maria? — Katie
4. Which two children caught the same number of fish? — Maria and Jordan
5. How many fish did Juan and Jordan catch altogether? — 7
6. Who caught one fish more than Maria? — Juan
7. How many fish did the children catch in all? — 12

66

Two-Digit Addition with Regrouping

To add some numbers, you must regroup.

Find each sum. Remember to regroup.

A. 14 +18 = 32   B. 62 +19 = 81   C. 38 +47 = 85   D. 68 +18 = 86   E. 25 +48 = 73

R-Controlled Vowel ir

Read these ir words. Use the words to answer the questions.

bird   first   girl   twirl   third

1. What is the opposite of boy? — girl
2. What grade comes after second? — third
3. What do you do with a baton? — twirl
4. What's another word for "number one"? — first
5. What animal builds its nest in a tree? — bird

67

R-Controlled Vowel ur

Read these ur words. Use the words to complete the sentences.

Burn   Turn   turtle   turkey   nurse

1. A nurse is a person who helps sick people.
2. Burn means what a fire does.
3. A turtle is an animal with a shell.
4. Turn the steering wheel.
5. The turkey says, "Gobble, gobble."

Double-Digit Regrouping

Check the addition in each number sentence below. Draw a √ in the box if the sum is correct. Draw an X in the box if the sum is not correct.

A. 35 +27 = 62 √   B. 68 +15 = 83 √   C. 29 +13 = 42 √   D. 35 +46 = 81 √

E. 51 +29 = 70 X   F. 37 +36 = 63 X   G. 42 +18 = 60 √   H. 55 +27 = 82 √

BONUS Add together the two smallest sums from this page. What is your answer? — 102

68

Measuring in Inches

Measure in inches from dot to dot. Add the numbers to find each answer.

1. = 4 in.
2. = 7 in.
3. = 6 in.
4. = 5 in.

Long ī

Circle the pictures that have the ī sound.

Write four more words that have the ī sound.

Answers will vary.

69

Long ō

Circle the words that have the ō vowel sound.

nose   crop
vote   cone   joke
pop   rope

Color the pictures that have the ō vowel sound.

Draw a picture of something that has the ō vowel sound in its name.

Pictures will vary.

Measuring in Centimeters

Measure in centimeters from dot to dot. Add the numbers to find each answer.

1.   2.   3.   4.

11 cm   12 cm   17 cm   22 cm

70

Greater Than, Less Than, or Equal To

The symbol < means less than.   12 < 17 (12 is less than 17)
The symbol = means equal to.   14 = 14 (14 is equal to 14)
The symbol > means greater than.   15 > 11 (15 is greater than 11)

Write the correct symbol (<, =, >) in each box to compare the numbers.

A. 16 > 12   B. 17 > 11   C. 15 = 15
D. 13 = 13   E. 15 < 16   F. 13 < 14
G. 18 > 15   H. 14 < 20   I. 17 > 15

Sequencing Events

Number the sentences in each group 1–4 to show the correct order.

1 Sharon came home from school.
3 Sharon made a sandwich.
4 Sharon ate a sandwich.
2 Sharon went to the kitchen.

1 Brooke chased lightning bugs.
4 The jar broke and the bugs flew away.
2 She caught two lightning bugs.
3 Brooke put the lightning bugs in a jar.

71

151

Answer Key

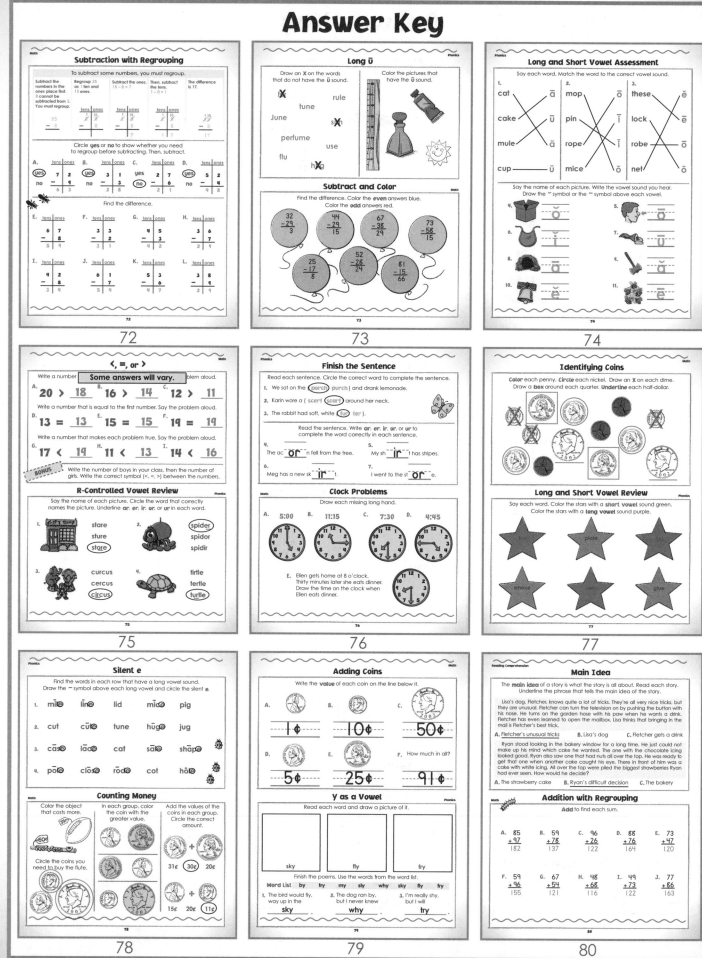

Subtraction with Regrouping

To subtract some numbers, you must regroup.

| Subtract the numbers in the ones place first. 8 cannot be subtracted from 5. You must regroup. | Regroup 25 as 1 ten and 15 ones. | Subtract the ones. 15 − 8 = 7 | Then, subtract the tens. 1 − 0 = 1 | The difference is 17. |

Circle **yes** or **no** to show whether you need to regroup before subtracting. Then, subtract.

A. **yes** / no — 7 2 − 9 = 6 3
B. **yes** / no — 3 1 − 3 = 2 8
C. yes / **no** — 2 7 − 6 = 2 1
D. **yes** / no — 5 2 − 4 = 4 8

Find the difference.

E. 6 − 8 = 5 8
F. 3 3 − 2 = 3 1
G. 4 5 − 3 = 4 2
H. 3 6 − 7 = 2 9

I. 4 2 − 8 = 3 4
J. 6 1 − 7 = 5 4
K. 5 3 − 6 = 4 7
L. 3 8 − 9 = 2 9

Page 72

Long ū

Draw an **X** on the words that do not have the ū sound.

i**X** rule
tune
June s**X**n
perfume use
flu h**X**g

Color the pictures that have the ū sound.

Subtract and Color

Find the difference. Color the **even** answers blue. Color the **odd** answers red.

32 − 29 = 3
44 − 29 = 15
67 − 38 = 29
73 − 58 = 15
25 − 17 = 8
52 − 28 = 24
81 − 15 = 66

Page 73

Long and Short Vowel Assessment

Say each word. Match the word to the correct vowel sound.

1. cat — ā, cake — ū, mule — ă, cup — ū
2. mop — ō, pin — ī, rope — ĭ, mice — ŏ
3. these — ē, lock — ē, robe — ō, net — ō

Say the name of each picture. Write the vowel sound you hear. Draw the ˘ symbol or the ¯ symbol above each vowel.

4. ŏ 5. ō
6. ĭ 7. ū
8. ā 9. (blank)
10. ĕ 11. ē

Page 74

<, =, or >

Write a number that makes each problem true. Say the problem aloud.

Some answers will vary.

A. 20 > 18
B. 16 > 14
C. 12 > 11

Write a number that is equal to the first number. Say the problem aloud.

D. 13 = 13
E. 15 = 15
F. 19 = 19

Write a number that makes each problem true. Say the problem aloud.

G. 17 < 19
H. 11 < 13
I. 14 < 16

BONUS Write the number of boys in your class, then the number of girls. Write the correct symbol (<, =, >) between the numbers.

R-Controlled Vowel Review

Say the name of each picture. Circle the word that correctly names the picture. Underline **ar, er, ir, or,** or **ur** in each word.

1. stare / sture / **store**
2. **spider** / spidor / spidir
3. curcus / cercus / **circus**
4. tirtle / tertle / **turtle**

Page 75

Finish the Sentence

Read each sentence. Circle the correct word to complete the sentence.

1. We sat on the (**porch** / purch) and drank lemonade.
2. Karin wore a (scerf / **scarf**) around her neck.
3. The rabbit had soft, white (**fur** / fer).

Read the sentence. Write **ar, er, ir, or,** or **ur** to complete the word correctly in each sentence.

4. The ac**or**n fell from the tree.
5. My sh**ir**t has stripes.
6. Meg has a new sk**ir**t.
7. I went to the st**or**e.

Clock Problems

Draw each missing long hand.

A. 5:00
B. 11:15
C. 7:30
D. 4:45

E. Ellen gets home at 8 o'clock. Thirty minutes later she eats dinner. Draw the time on the clock when Ellen eats dinner.

Page 76

Identifying Coins

Color each penny. **Circle** each nickel. Draw an **X** on each dime. Draw a **box** around each quarter. **Underline** each half-dollar.

Long and Short Vowel Review

Say each word. Color the stars with a **short vowel** sound green. Color the stars with a **long vowel** sound purple.

(stars: plate, smoke, glue)

Page 77

Silent e

Find the words in each row that have a long vowel sound. Draw the ¯ symbol above each long vowel and circle the silent **e**.

1. mīl**e** līn**e** lid mīc**e** pig
2. cut cūt**e** tune hūg**e** jug
3. cās**e** lāc**e** cat sāl**e** shāp**e**
4. pōl**e** clōs**e** rōd**e** cot hōl**e**

Counting Money

Color the object that costs more. / In each group, color the coin with the greater value. / Add the values of the coins in each group. Circle the correct amount.

Circle the coins you need to buy the flute.

31¢ (30¢) 20¢
15¢ 20¢ (11¢)

Page 78

Adding Coins

Write the **value** of each coin on the line below it.

A. 1¢
B. 10¢
C. 50¢
D. 5¢
E. 25¢
F. How much in all? 91¢

Y as a Vowel

Read each word and draw a picture of it.

sky fly fry

Finish the poems. Use the words from the word list.

Word List by try my sly why sky fly fry

1. The bird would fly, way up in the **sky**
2. The dog ran by, but I never knew **why**
3. I'm really shy, but I will **try**

Page 79

Main Idea

The **main idea** of a story is what the story is all about. Read each story. Underline the phrase that tells the main idea of the story.

Lisa's dog, Fletcher, knows quite a lot of tricks. They're all very nice tricks, but they are unusual. Fletcher can turn the television on by pushing the button with his nose. He turns on the garden hose with his paw when he wants a drink. Fletcher has even learned to open the mailbox. Lisa thinks that bringing in the mail is Fletcher's best trick.

A. Fletcher's unusual tricks   B. Lisa's dog   C. Fletcher gets a drink

Ryan stood looking in the bakery window for a long time. He just could not make up his mind which cake he wanted. The one with the chocolate icing looked good. Ryan also saw one that had nuts all over the top. He was ready to get that one when another cake caught his eye. There in front of him was a cake with white icing. All over the top were piled the biggest strawberries Ryan had ever seen. How would he decide?

A. The strawberry cake   B. Ryan's difficult decision   C. The bakery

Addition with Regrouping

Add to find each sum.

A. 85 + 97 = 182
B. 59 + 78 = 137
C. 96 + 26 = 122
D. 88 + 76 = 164
E. 73 + 47 = 120

F. 59 + 96 = 155
G. 67 + 54 = 121
H. 48 + 68 = 116
I. 49 + 73 = 122
J. 77 + 86 = 163

Page 80

Answer Key

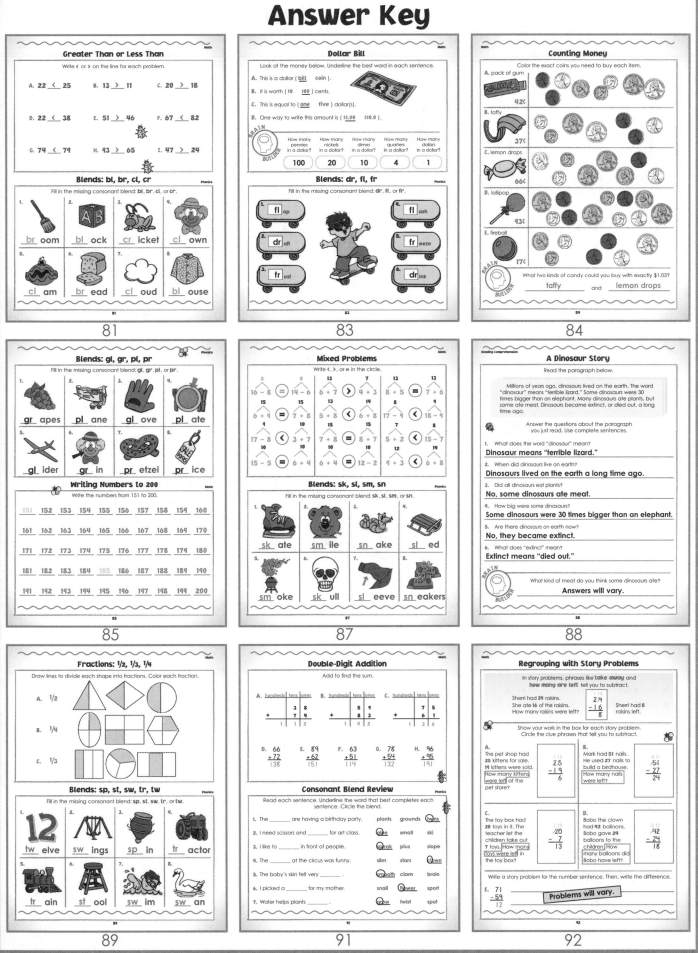

Greater Than or Less Than
Write < or > on the line for each problem.

A. 22 < 25   B. 13 > 11   C. 20 > 18

D. 22 < 38   E. 51 > 46   F. 67 < 82

G. 74 < 79   H. 93 > 65   I. 47 > 24

Blends: bl, br, cl, cr
Fill in the missing consonant blend: bl, br, cl, or cr.

1. br oom 2. bl ock 3. cr icket 4. cl own
5. cl am 6. br ead 7. cl oud 8. bl ouse

Dollar Bill
Look at the money below. Underline the best word in each sentence.

A. This is a dollar (bill coin).
B. It is worth (10 100) cents.
C. This is equal to (one five) dollar(s).
D. One way to write this amount is ($1.00 $10.0).

How many pennies in a dollar? **100**
How many nickels in a dollar? **20**
How many dimes in a dollar? **10**
How many quarters in a dollar? **4**
How many dollars in a dollar? **1**

Blends: dr, fl, fr
Fill in the missing consonant blend: dr, fl, or fr.

1. fl ap 2. dr aft 3. fr ost 4. fl ash 5. fr eeze 6. dr ink

Counting Money
Color the exact coins you need to buy each item.

A. pack of gum 42¢
B. taffy 37¢
C. lemon drops 66¢
D. lollipop 93¢
E. fireball 17¢

What two kinds of candy could you buy with exactly $1.03?
taffy and **lemon drops**

Blends: gl, gr, pl, pr
Fill in the missing consonant blend: gl, gr, pl, or pr.

1. gr apes 2. pl ane 3. gl ove 4. pl ate
5. gl ider 6. gr in 7. pr etzel 8. pr ice

Writing Numbers to 200
Write the numbers from 151 to 200.

151	152	153	154	155	156	157	158	159	160
161	162	163	164	165	166	167	168	169	170
171	172	173	174	175	176	177	178	179	180
181	182	183	184	185	186	187	188	189	190
191	192	193	194	195	196	197	198	199	200

Mixed Problems
Write <, >, or = in the circle.

16 − 8 = 14 − 6   13 > 7   13 = 13
15 = 15   13 < 14   8 < 9
6 + 9 = 7 + 8   5 + 8 < 6 + 8   17 − 4 = 18 − 4
9 < 15   15 > 7   8 < 9
17 − 4 < 3 + 7   7 + 8 = 8 + 7   5 + 2 < 15 − 7
10 = 10   10 = 10   12 = 14
15 − 5 = 6 + 4   6 + 4 = 12 − 2   9 + 3 < 6 + 8

Blends: sk, sl, sm, sn
Fill in the missing consonant blend: sk, sl, sm, or sn.

1. sk ate 2. sm ile 3. sn ake 4. sl ed
5. sm oke 6. sk ull 7. sl eeve 8. sn eakers

A Dinosaur Story
Read the paragraph below.

Millions of years ago, dinosaurs lived on the earth. The word "dinosaur" means "terrible lizard." Some dinosaurs were 30 times bigger than an elephant. Many dinosaurs ate plants, but some ate meat. Dinosaurs became extinct, or died out, a long time ago.

Answer the questions about the paragraph you just read. Use complete sentences.

1. What does the word "dinosaur" mean?
Dinosaur means "terrible lizard."
2. When did dinosaurs live on earth?
Dinosaurs lived on the earth a long time ago.
3. Did all dinosaurs eat plants?
No, some dinosaurs ate meat.
4. How big were some dinosaurs?
Some dinosaurs were 30 times bigger than an elephant.
5. Are there dinosaurs on earth now?
No, they became extinct.
6. What does "extinct" mean?
Extinct means "died out."

What kind of meat do you think some dinosaurs ate?
Answers will vary.

Fractions: 1/2, 1/3, 1/4
Draw lines to divide each shape into fractions. Color each fraction.

A. 1/2
B. 1/4
C. 1/3

Blends: sp, st, sw, tr, tw
Fill in the missing consonant blend: sp, st, sw, tr, or tw.

1. tw elve 2. sw ings 3. sp in 4. tr actor
5. tr ain 6. st ool 7. sw im 8. sw an

Double-Digit Addition
Add to find the sum.

A.	hundreds	tens	ones		B.	hundreds	tens	ones		C.	hundreds	tens	ones
		3	8				5	9				7	5
	+	7	4			+	8	3			+	6	1
	1	1	2			1	4	2			1	3	6

D. 66 +72 = 138
E. 89 +62 = 151
F. 63 +51 = 114
G. 78 +54 = 132
H. 96 +95 = 191

Consonant Blend Review
Read each sentence. Underline the word that best completes each sentence. Circle the blend.

1. The _____ are having a birthday party. plants grounds (twins)
2. I need scissors and _____ for art class. (glue) small ski
3. I like to _____ in front of people. (speak) plus slope
4. The _____ at the circus was funny. slim stars (clown)
5. The baby's skin felt very _____. (smooth) clam brain
6. I picked a _____ for my mother. snail (flower) sport
7. Water helps plants _____. (grow) twist spot

Regrouping with Story Problems
In story problems, phrases like **take away** and **how many are left** tell you to subtract.

Sherri had 24 raisins. She ate 16 of the raisins. How many raisins were left?
1 14
2 4
− 1 6
8
Sherri had 8 raisins left.

Show your work in the box for each story problem. Circle the clue phrases that tell you to subtract.

A. The pet shop had 25 kittens for sale. 19 kittens were sold. How many were left at the pet store?
1 15
2 5
− 1 9
6

B. Mark had 51 nails. He used 27 nails to build a birdhouse. How many nails were left?
4 11
5 1
− 2 7
2 4

C. The toy box had 20 toys in it. The teacher let the children take out 7 toys. How many toys were left in the toy box?
1 10
2 0
− 7
1 3

D. Bobo the clown had 42 balloons. Bobo gave 24 balloons to the children. How many balloons did Bobo have left?
3 12
4 2
− 2 4
1 8

Write a story problem for the number sentence. Then, write the difference.

E. 71 −59 = 12   **Problems will vary.**

Answer Key

Consonant Blend Assessment

Circle the beginning blend in each word.

1. **cl**uck   2. **gr**ape   3. **sh**ake   4. **st**em   5. **sl**ip
6. **sl**ed   7. **cr**own   8. **sm**ile   9. **sk**ate   10. **sn**ail
11. **fl**ame   12. **cr**own   13. **sw**ing   14. **sp**ider   15. **tw**ig
16. **pl**ant   17. **sh**ush   18. **th**in   19. **fl**ower   20. **pr**etzel

Say the name of each picture.
Circle the blend you hear at the beginning of the word.

21. **bl**   22. br **tr** fl   23. cr fr **pr**
24. **sw** tr tw   25. pl **fr** st   26. pr gl **sn**
27. **dr** gl sp   28. sk **tr** sl   29. sm cr **sk**

Write the correct compound word next to each set of pictures.
Circle the blend in each compound word.

30. tooth**br**ush
31. fire**fl**y

93

Break the Code

Subtract. Remember to regroup. Use the code to solve the riddle.

What did dinosaurs have that no other animal has ever had?

46	25	64	37	47	19	44	28	58	17
D	B	N	A	R	U	S	Y	O	I

53	71	84	46
-28	-34	-59	-18
25	37	25	28
B	A	B	Y

63	75	92	84	63	96	37	66	65
-17	-58	-28	-26	-14	-59	-18	-19	-16
46	17	64	58	49	37	19	47	49
D	I	N	O	S	A	U	R	S

Rewrite in column form. Regroup and subtract.

A. 83 - 68 =
83
-68
15

B. 44 - 27 =
44
-27
17

94

Regrouping with Three Addends

| To find the sum of three addends... | Add the ones first. 8 + 7 + 9 = 24 24 = 2 tens and 4 ones | Write the 4 in the ones place. Regroup the 2 into the tens place. | Add the tens. 2 + 1 + 2 + 1 = 6 | The sum is 64. |

Find the sum of the three addends. Be sure to regroup.

A. 22
14
+36
72

B. 68
12
+6
86

C. 29
18
+24
71

D. 61
5
+14
80

E. 21
32
+18
71

Descriptive Sentences

A **descriptive sentence** tells details about something.

The loud, black dog barked at the pretty lady.

Write a descriptive sentence about each topic below.

1. a white cloud
2. a sad giraffe
3. a yellow taxi   **Sentences will vary.**
4. the small mouse

95

Main Idea

Read each story. Choose the phrase that tells the main idea of the story.
Write the letter of the correct phrase in the box.

For a monkey, Cici wasn't doing badly at all. Still, the zookeeper thought she should learn some new tricks. Cici was sent to gymnastics classes. So far, Cici has learned to swing from the rings quite well, and she can almost walk across the balance beam. Cici's teacher wants her to learn to do some stunts on the trampoline, too. Cici thinks that swinging, bouncing, and jumping were all easier in the jungle!

A. Cici takes gymnastic lessons
B. A monkey with a good home   **A**
C. Cici and the zookeeper

Regrouping with Three Addends

Find the sums. Remember to regroup.

A. 35
16
+22
73

B. 7
24
+36
67

C. 51
12
+27
90

D. 68
23
+3
94

E. 25
48
+3
76

Rewrite each number sentence vertically in the box.
Then, add to find the sum.

F. 12
26
+25
63

G. 15
18
+23
47

H. 21
18
+43
82

12 + 26 + 25 = _63_
15 + 9 + 23 = _47_
21 + 18 + 43 = _82_

96

Consonant Digraphs: ch, sh, th

Read the words in the word list. Write each word below its beginning digraph.

Word List: chip, shy, thumb, thin, chin, ship, thick, sheep, chunk

1. ch — chip, chin, chunk
2. sh — shy, ship, sheep
3. th — thumb, thin, thick

Writing Descriptive Sentences

1. Write a descriptive sentence about something in your house.
2. Write a descriptive sentence about a friend.   **Sentences will vary.**
3. Write a descriptive sentence about an animal.

97

Quotation Marks

Quotation marks (" ") are placed around words people say in a sentence.

Mr. Ving said, "Good morning, class."

In each sentence, underline the exact words spoken by the person.
Put quotation marks around the quotation.

1. Frank said to Paula, "I enjoyed playing with you today."
2. "I hope I can go to the party," said Derek.
3. "This pizza is delicious!" exclaimed Chris.
4. William saw the ice cream and said to his mom, "May I have some, please?"

Consonant Digraphs: ch, sh, th

Say the name of each picture. Circle its beginning sound.

ch **sh** th   ch sh **sh**   **ch** sh th
ch **sh** th   ch **sh** th   ch **sh** th
ch **sh** th   **ch** sh th   ch **sh** th

98

Finish the Patterns

Draw lines to continue each pattern.

Consonant Digraph -ng

Read each sentence and the words below it.
Write the **ng** word that completes each sentence.

1. I like to **sing** in music class.
   bring sing ding
2. I'm sorry, but that answer is **wrong**
   wrong song long

Write the **ng** digraph at the end of each set of letters. Say the words.

3. cla**ng**   4. wro**ng**   5. bri**ng**   6. si**ng**

99

Checking Subtraction with Addition

| To check subtraction with addition... | Add the difference to the amount that was subtracted. | This sum should equal the first number from the subtraction sentence. |

Draw a line from each subtraction problem to the checking problem.

A. 62
-36
26 → 26
+36
62

B. 82
-7
75 → 40
+16
56

C. 56
-16
40 → 18
+19
37

D. 37
-19
18 → 75
+7
82

Solve each subtraction problem.
Check your work with addition.

E. 83
-17
66 → 66
+17
83

F. 50
-25
25 → 25
+25
50

G. 46
-18
28 → 28
+18
46

H. 57
-38
19 → 19
+38
57

BONUS Read the addition problem to the right.
Use the numbers to write a subtraction problem.

36
+18
54

54
-18
36

100

Hundred Chart

Write the numbers to complete the hundred chart.

1	2	3	4	5	6	7	8	9	10
11	12	13	14	15	16	17	18	19	20
21	22	23	24	25	26	27	28	29	30
31	32	33	34	35	36	37	38	39	40
41	42	43	44	45	46	47	48	49	50
51	52	53	54	55	56	57	58	59	60
61	62	63	64	65	66	67	68	69	70
71	72	73	74	75	76	77	78	79	80
81	82	83	84	85	86	87	88	89	90
91	92	93	94	95	96	97	98	99	100

Time yourself. How fast can you count to 100?

101

Answer Key

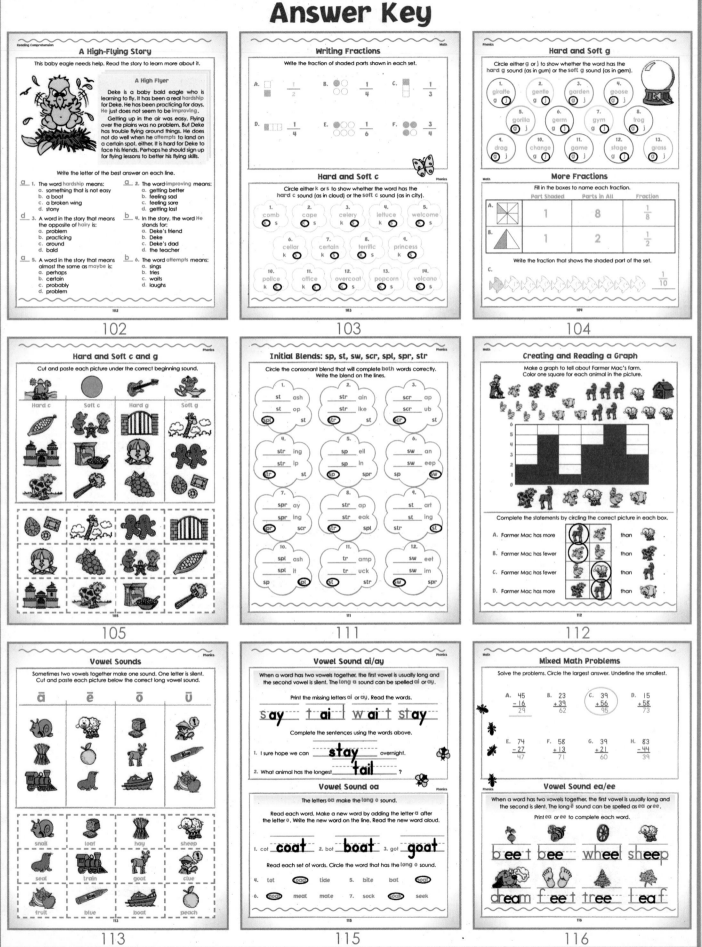

Answer Key

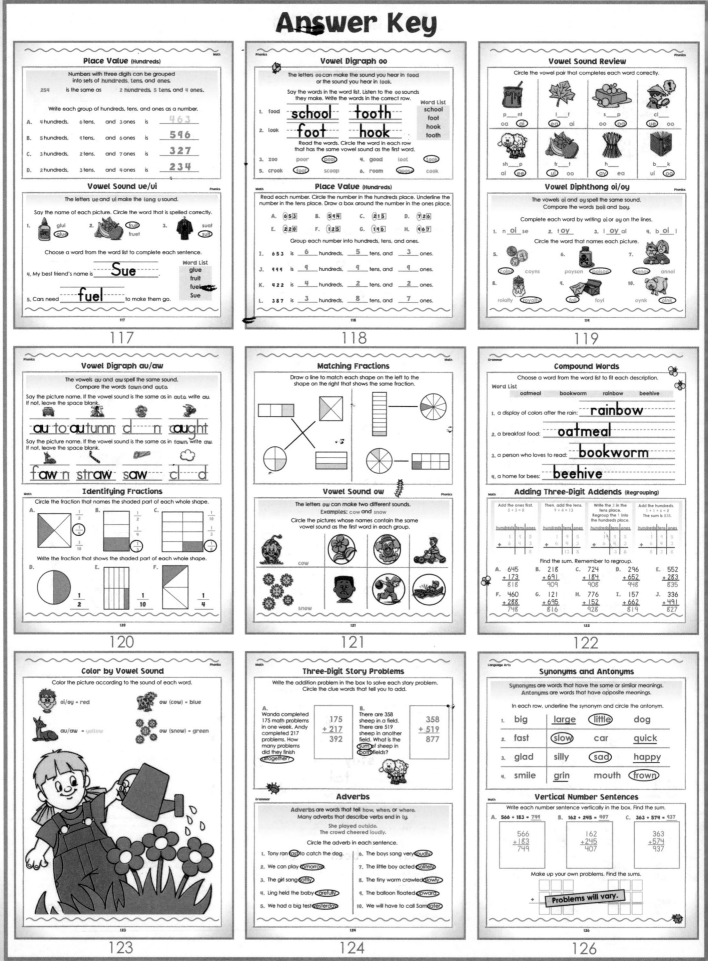

Place Value (Hundreds)

Numbers with three digits can be grouped into sets of hundreds, tens, and ones.

254 is the same as 2 hundreds, 5 tens, and 4 ones.

Write each group of hundreds, tens, and ones as a number.

A. 4 hundreds, 6 tens, and 3 ones is 463
B. 5 hundreds, 9 tens, and 6 ones is 596
C. 3 hundreds, 2 tens, and 7 ones is 327
D. 2 hundreds, 3 tens, and 4 ones is 234

Vowel Sound ue/ui

The letters ue and ui make the long u sound.

Say the name of each picture. Circle the word that is spelled correctly.

1. glui / (glue)
2. (fruit) / fruet
3. suat / (suit)

Choose a word from the word list to complete each sentence.

4. My best friend's name is Sue

5. Cars need fuel to make them go.

Word List: glue, fruit, fuel, Sue

117

Vowel Digraph oo

The letters oo can make the sound you hear in food or the sound you hear in look.

Say the words in the word list. Listen to the oo sounds they make. Write the words in the correct row.

1. food — school tooth
2. look — foot hook

Word List: school, foot, hook, tooth

Read the words. Circle the word in each row that has the same vowel sound as the first word.

3. zoo — poor (pool)
4. good — loot (look)
5. crook — (foot) scoop
6. room — (zoom) cook

Place Value (Hundreds)

Read each number. Circle the number in the hundreds place. Underline the number in the tens place. Draw a box around the number in the ones place.

A. (6)53 B. (5)94 C. (2)15 D. (7)26
E. (2)20 F. (1)25 G. (1)96 H. (9)67

Group each number into hundreds, tens, and ones.

I. 653 is 6 hundreds, 5 tens, and 3 ones.
J. 999 is 9 hundreds, 9 tens, and 9 ones.
K. 422 is 4 hundreds, 2 tens, and 2 ones.
L. 387 is 3 hundreds, 8 tens, and 7 ones.

118

Vowel Sound Review

Circle the vowel pair that completes each word correctly.

p_nt: oa (ai)   l_f: (ea) ai   s_p: oo (oo)   cl__: (ue) oo
sh_p: ai (ee)   fr_t: (ui) oo h_: (oy) ea   b_k: ui (oo)

Vowel Diphthong oi/oy

The vowels oi and oy spell the same sound. Compare the words boil and boy.

Complete each word by writing oi or oy on the lines.

1. n oi se   2. t oy   3. l oy al   4. b oi l

Circle the word that names each picture.

5. (coins) coyns
6. poyson (poison)
7. (annoi) annoi
8. rolalty (royalty)
9. (toil) toyl
10. oynk (oink)

119

Vowel Digraph au/aw

The vowels au and aw spell the same sound. Compare the words fawn and auto.

Say the picture name. If the vowel sound is the same as in auto, write au. If not, leave the space blank.

au to   autumn   d___n   caught

Say the picture name. If the vowel sound is the same as in fawn, write aw. If not, leave the space blank.

faw n   straw   saw   cl__d

Identifying Fractions

Circle the fraction that names the shaded part of each whole shape.

A. 1/2 (1/2) 1/10   B. 1/2 (1/4) 1/4   C. 1/10 (1/3) 1/3

Write the fraction that shows the shaded part of each whole shape.

D. 1/2   E. 1/10   F. 1/4

120

Matching Fractions

Draw a line to match each shape on the left to the shape on the right that shows the same fraction.

Vowel Sound ow

The letters ow can make two different sounds.
Examples: cow and snow

Circle the pictures whose names contain the same vowel sound as the first word in each group.

cow

snow

121

Compound Words

Choose a word from the word list to fit each description.

Word List: oatmeal, bookworm, rainbow, beehive

1. a display of colors after the rain: rainbow
2. a breakfast food: oatmeal
3. a person who loves to read: bookworm
4. a home for bees: beehive

Adding Three-Digit Addends (Regrouping)

Add the ones first. 5 + 3 = 8
Then, add the tens. 9 + 4 = 13
Write the 3 in the tens place. Regroup the 1 into the hundreds place. The sum is 838.
Add the hundreds. 1 + 1 + 6 = 8 The sum is 838.

Find the sum. Remember to regroup.

A. 645 + 173 = 818
B. 218 + 691 = 909
C. 724 + 184 = 908
D. 296 + 652 = 948
E. 552 + 283 = 835
F. 460 + 288 = 748
G. 121 + 695 = 816
H. 776 + 152 = 928
I. 157 + 662 = 819
J. 336 + 491 = 827

122

Color by Vowel Sound

Color the picture according to the sound of each word.

oi/oy = red
ow (cow) = blue
au/aw = yellow
ow (snow) = green

123

Three-Digit Story Problems

Write the addition problem in the box to solve each story problem. Circle the clue words that tell you to add.

A. Wanda completed 175 math problems in one week. Andy completed 217 problems. How many problems did they finish (altogether)?
175 + 217 = 392

B. There are 358 sheep in a field. There are 519 sheep in another field. What is the (sum) of sheep in (both) fields?
358 + 519 = 877

Adverbs

Adverbs are words that tell how, when, or where. Many adverbs that describe verbs end in ly.

She played outside.
The crowd cheered loudly.

Circle the adverb in each sentence.

1. Tony ran (fast) to catch the dog.
2. We can play (tomorrow).
3. The girl sang (softly).
4. Ling held the baby (carefully).
5. We had a big test (yesterday).
6. The boys sang very (loudly).
7. The little boy acted (politely).
8. The tiny worm crawled (slowly).
9. The balloon floated (upward).
10. We will have to call Sam (later).

124

Synonyms and Antonyms

Synonyms are words that have the same or similar meanings. Antonyms are words that have opposite meanings.

In each row, underline the synonym and circle the antonym.

1. big — large (little) dog
2. fast — (slow) car quick
3. glad — silly (sad) happy
4. smile — grin mouth (frown)

Vertical Number Sentences

Write each number sentence vertically in the box. Find the sum.

A. 566 + 183 = 749
566 + 183 = 749

B. 162 + 245 = 407
162 + 245 = 407

C. 363 + 574 = 937
363 + 574 = 937

Make up your own problems. Find the sums.

Problems will vary.

126

Answer Key

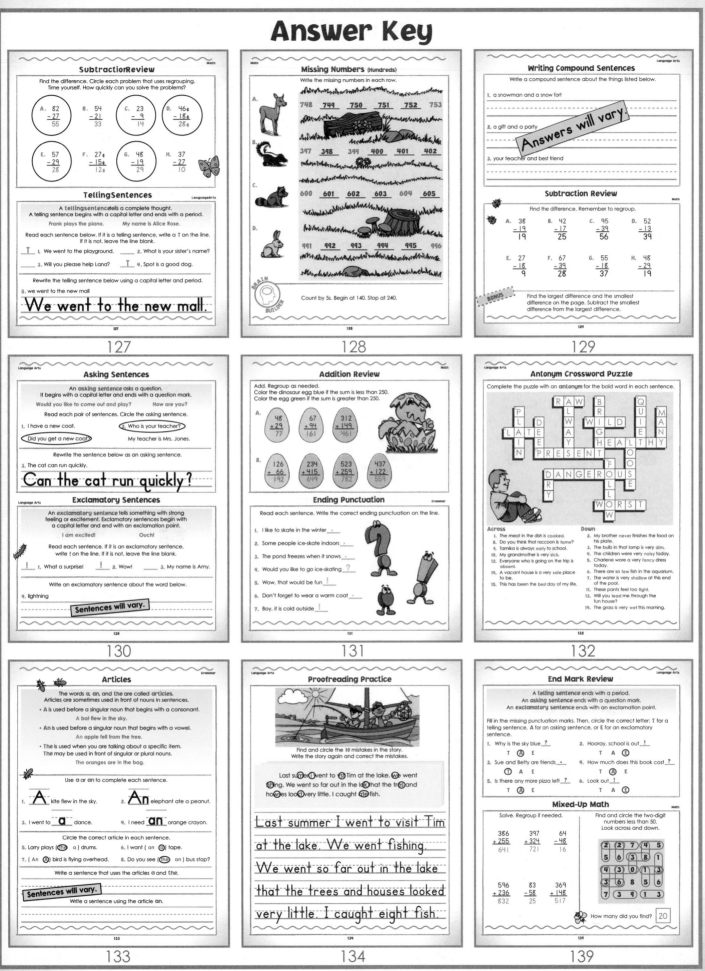

Subtraction Review
Math

Find the difference. Circle each problem that uses regrouping.
Time yourself. How quickly can you solve the problems?

A. 82 − 27 = 55   B. 54 − 21 = 33   C. 23 − 9 = 14   D. 46¢ − 18¢ = 28¢

E. 57 − 29 = 28   F. 27¢ − 15¢ = 12¢   G. 48 − 19 = 29   H. 37 − 27 = 10

Telling Sentences
Language Arts

A **telling sentence** tells a complete thought.
A telling sentence begins with a capital letter and ends with a period.

Frank plays the piano.   My name is Alice Rose.

Read each sentence below. If it is a telling sentence, write a T on the line.
If it is not, leave the line blank.

T 1. We went to the playground.   ___ 2. What is your sister's name?

___ 3. Will you please help Lana?   **T** 4. Spot is a good dog.

Rewrite the telling sentence below using a capital letter and period.

5. we went to the new mall

We went to the new mall.

127

Missing Numbers (Hundreds)
Math

Write the missing numbers in each row.

A. 748 **749** 750 751 **752** 753

B. 397 **398** 399 **400** **401** **402**

C. 600 **601** **602** **603** 604 **605**

D. 991 **992** **993** **994** **995** **996**

Count by 5s. Begin at 140. Stop at 240.

128

Writing Compound Sentences
Language Arts

Write a compound sentence about the things listed below.

1. a snowman and a snow fort

2. a gift and a party

Answers will vary.

3. your teacher and best friend

Subtraction Review
Math

Find the difference. Remember to regroup.

A. 38 − 19 = 19   B. 42 − 17 = 25   C. 95 − 39 = 56   D. 52 − 13 = 39

E. 27 − 18 = 9   F. 67 − 39 = 28   G. 55 − 18 = 37   H. 48 − 29 = 19

BONUS Find the largest difference and the smallest difference on the page. Subtract the smallest difference from the largest difference.

129

Asking Sentences
Language Arts

An **asking sentence** asks a question.
It begins with a capital letter and ends with a question mark.

Would you like to come out and play?   How are you?

Read each pair of sentences. Circle the asking sentence.

1. I have a new coat.   (2. Who is your teacher?)

(Did you get a new coat?)   My teacher is Mrs. Jones.

Rewrite the sentence below as an asking sentence.

3. The cat can run quickly.

Can the cat run quickly?

Exclamatory Sentences
Language Arts

An **exclamatory sentence** tells something with strong feeling or excitement. Exclamatory sentences begin with a capital letter and end with an exclamation point.

I am excited!   Ouch!

Read each sentence. If it is an exclamatory sentence, write ! on the line. If it is not, leave the line blank.

! 1. What a surprise!   **!** 2. Wow!   ___ 3. My name is Amy.

Write an exclamatory sentence about the word below.

4. lightning

Sentences will vary.

130

Addition Review
Math

Add. Regroup as needed.
Color the dinosaur egg blue if the sum is less than 250.
Color the egg green if the sum is greater than 250.

A. 48 + 29 = 77   67 + 94 = 161   312 + 149 = 461

B. 126 + 66 = 192   234 + 415 = 649   523 + 259 = 782   437 + 122 = 559

Ending Punctuation
Grammar

Read each sentence. Write the correct ending punctuation on the line.

1. I like to skate in the winter .

2. Some people ice-skate indoors .

3. The pond freezes when it snows .

4. Would you like to go ice-skating ?

5. Wow, that would be fun !

6. Don't forget to wear a warm coat .

7. Boy, it is cold outside !

131

Antonym Crossword Puzzle
Language Arts

Complete the puzzle with an **antonym** for the bold word in each sentence.

Across:
RAW, WILD, LATE, PRESENT, HEALTHY, DANGEROUS, WORST
Down:
PLAIN, ALWAYS, QUIET, MANY, LOOSE, DRY, FEW, FULL

Across
1. The meat in the dish is **cooked**.
8. Do you think that raccoon is **tame**?
4. Tamika is always **early** to school.
10. My grandmother is very **sick**.
12. Everyone who is going on the trip is **absent**.
14. A vacant house is a very **safe** place to be.
15. This has been the best day of my life.

Down
2. My brother never finishes the food on his plate.
3. The bulb in that lamp is very dim.
4. The children were very noisy today.
5. Charlene wore a very fancy dress today.
6. There are so few fish in the aquarium.
7. The water is very shallow at this end of the pool.
11. These pants feel too tight.
13. Will you lead me through the fun house?
14. The grass is very wet this morning.

132

Articles
Grammar

The words **a**, **an**, and **the** are called **articles**.
Articles are sometimes used in front of nouns in sentences.

• **A** is used before a singular noun that begins with a consonant.
  A bat flew in the sky.

• **An** is used before a singular noun that begins with a vowel.
  An apple fell from the tree.

• **The** is used when you are talking about a specific item.
  The may be used in front of singular or plural nouns.
  The oranges are in the bag.

Use **a** or **an** to complete each sentence.

1. **A** kite flew in the sky.   2. **An** elephant ate a peanut.

3. I went to **a** dance.   4. I need **an** orange crayon.

Circle the correct article in each sentence.

5. Larry plays (the) a) drums.   6. I want (an (a)) tape.

7. (An (a)) bird is flying overhead.   8. Do you see (the) an) bus stop?

Write a sentence that uses the articles a and the.

Sentences will vary.

Write a sentence using the article an.

133

Proofreading Practice
Language Arts

Find and circle the 10 mistakes in the story.
Write the story again and correct the mistakes.

Last summer i went to vsit Tim at the lake. we went fihing. We went so far out in the laek that the trees and houses look very little. I caught ate fish.

Last summer I went to visit Tim at the lake. We went fishing. We went so far out in the lake that the trees and houses looked very little. I caught eight fish.

134

End Mark Review
Language Arts

A **telling sentence** ends with a period.
An **asking sentence** ends with a question mark.
An **exclamatory sentence** ends with an exclamation point.

Fill in the missing punctuation marks. Then, circle the correct letter; T for a telling sentence, A for an asking sentence, or E for an exclamatory sentence.

1. Why is the sky blue ?   2. Hooray, school is out !
   T (A) E   T A (E)

3. Sue and Betty are friends .   4. How much does this book cost ?
   (T) A E   T (A) E

5. Is there any more pizza left ?   6. Look out !
   T (A) E   T A (E)

Mixed-Up Math
Math

Solve. Regroup if needed.

386 + 255 = 641   397 + 324 = 721   64 − 48 = 16

596 + 236 = 832   83 − 58 = 25   369 + 148 = 517

Find and circle the two-digit numbers less than 50. Look across and down.

How many did you find? **20**

134

157

Answer Key

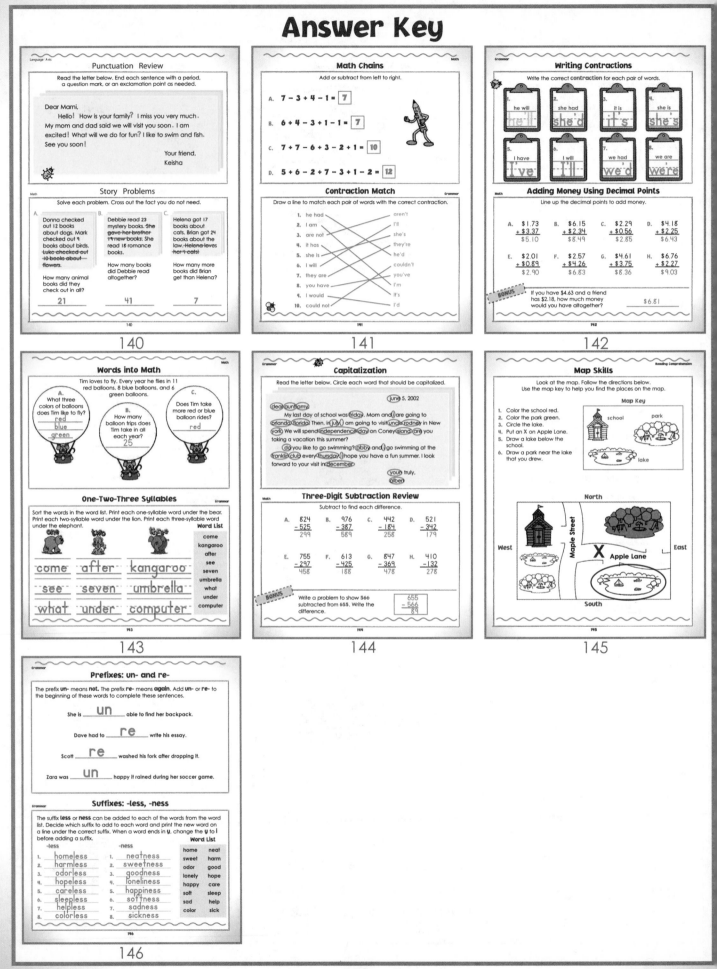

Punctuation Review
Language Arts

Read the letter below. End each sentence with a period, a question mark, or an exclamation point as needed.

Dear Marni,
Hello! How is your family? I miss you very much. My mom and dad said we will visit you soon. I am excited! What will we do for fun? I like to swim and fish. See you soon!

Your friend,
Keisha

Story Problems
Math

Solve each problem. Cross out the fact you do not need.

A. Donna checked out 12 books about dogs. Mark checked out 9 books about birds. ~~Luke checked out 10 books about flowers.~~

How many animal books did they check out in all?

21

B. Debbie read 23 mystery books. ~~She gave her brother 14 new books.~~ She read 18 romance books.

How many books did Debbie read altogether?

41

C. Helena got 17 books about cats. Brian got 24 books about the law. ~~Helena loves her 4 cats!~~

How many more books did Brian get than Helena?

7

140

Math Chains
Math

Add or subtract from left to right.

A. 7 − 3 + 4 − 1 = **7**

B. 6 + 4 − 3 + 1 − 1 = **7**

C. 7 + 7 − 6 + 3 − 2 + 1 = **10**

D. 5 + 6 − 2 + 7 − 3 + 1 − 2 = **12**

Contraction Match
Grammar

Draw a line to match each pair of words with the correct contraction.

1. he had — he'd
2. I am — I'm
3. are not — aren't
4. it has — it's
5. she is — she's
6. I will — I'll
7. they are — they're
8. you have — you've
9. I would — I'd
10. could not — couldn't

141

Writing Contractions
Grammar

Write the correct contraction for each pair of words.

1. he will — **he'll**
2. she had — **she'd**
3. it is — **it's**
4. she is — **she's**
5. I have — **I've**
6. I will — **I'll**
7. we had — **we'd**
8. we are — **were**

Adding Money Using Decimal Points
Math

Line up the decimal points to add money.

A. $1.73 + $3.37 = $5.10
B. $6.15 + $2.34 = $8.49
C. $2.29 + $0.56 = $2.85
D. $4.18 + $2.25 = $6.43
E. $2.01 + $0.89 = $2.90
F. $2.57 + $4.26 = $6.83
G. $4.61 + $3.75 = $8.36
H. $6.76 + $2.27 = $9.03

BONUS: If you have $4.63 and a friend has $2.18, how much money would you have altogether? $6.81

142

Words into Math
Math

Tim loves to fly. Every year he flies in 11 red balloons, 8 blue balloons, and 6 green balloons.

A. What three colors of balloons does Tim like to fly?
red
blue
green

B. How many balloon trips does Tim take in all each year?
25

C. Does Tim take more red or blue balloon rides?
red

One-Two-Three Syllables
Grammar

Sort the words in the word list. Print each one-syllable word under the bear. Print each two-syllable word under the lion. Print each three-syllable word under the elephant.

Word List
come
kangaroo
after
see
seven
umbrella
what
under
computer

one: come, see, what
two: after, seven, under
three: kangaroo, umbrella, computer

143

Capitalization
Grammar

Read the letter below. Circle each word that should be capitalized.

June 5, 2002

Dear Aunt Amy,
My last day of school was Friday. Mom and I are going to Orlando, Florida. Then, in July, I am going to visit Uncle Rodney in New York. We will spend Independence Day on Coney Island. Are you taking a vacation this summer?
Do you like to go swimming? Abby and I go swimming at the Franklin Club every Thursday. I hope you have a fun summer. I look forward to your visit in December.

Yours truly,
Albert

Three-Digit Subtraction Review
Math

Subtract to find each difference.

A. 824 − 525 = 299
B. 976 − 387 = 589
C. 442 − 184 = 258
D. 521 − 342 = 179
E. 755 − 297 = 458
F. 613 − 425 = 188
G. 847 − 369 = 478
H. 410 − 132 = 278

BONUS: Write a problem to show 566 subtracted from 655. Write the difference.
655 − 566 = 89

144

Map Skills
Reading Comprehension

Look at the map. Follow the directions below. Use the map key to help you find the places on the map.

1. Color the school red.
2. Color the park green.
3. Circle the lake.
4. Put an X on Apple Lane.
5. Draw a lake below the school.
6. Draw a park near the lake that you drew.

Map Key
school   park   lake

North   West   East   South
Maple Street   Apple Lane

145

Prefixes: un- and re-
Grammar

The prefix **un-** means **not.** The prefix **re-** means **again.** Add **un-** or **re-** to the beginning of these words to complete these sentences.

She is **un**able to find her backpack.

Dave had to **re**write his essay.

Scott **re**washed his fork after dropping it.

Zara was **un**happy it rained during her soccer game.

Suffixes: -less, -ness
Grammar

The suffix **less** or **ness** can be added to each of the words from the word list. Decide which suffix to add to each word and print the new word on a line under the correct suffix. When a word ends in **y**, change the **y** to **i** before adding a suffix.

Word List
home   neat
sweet   harm
odor   good
lonely   hope
happy   care
soft   sleep
sad   help
color   sick

-less
1. homeless
2. harmless
3. odorless
4. hopeless
5. careless
6. sleepless
7. helpless
8. colorless

-ness
1. neatness
2. sweetness
3. goodness
4. loneliness
5. happiness
6. softness
7. sadness
8. sickness

146

158

Cut-and-Color Awards

Parent: Have your child decorate and color these awards. Fill in your child's name and the date to mark each accomplishment. The awards can be worn as badges or put into small frames.

I can measure in inches and centimeters!

Name: _____ Date: _____

I can add and subtract with regrouping!

Name: _____ Date: _____

I can read and make graphs!

Name: _____ Date: _____

I know my fractions!

Name: _____ Date: _____

I can use contractions correctly!

Name: _____ Date: _____

nouns verbs adverbs

I know my parts of speech!

adjectives

Name: _____ Date: _____

I can use punctuation correctly!

Name: _____ Date: _____

I understand synonyms, homonyms, and antonyms!

Name: _____ Date: _____